THE ANGELS
OF ATLANTIS

Twelve Mighty Forces
to Transform Your Life Forever

D1009348

FINDHORN PRESS

Also by Stewart Pearce

BOOKS

The Alchemy of Voice
The Heart's Note

SET OF CARDS / iOS APP

Angels of Atlantis Oracle Cards

CDS/MP3S

The Alchemy of Voice – Awakening
The Alchemy of Voice – Initiation
Sonic Meditations

BOOK, SET OF CARDS AND MP3S
AVAILABLE FROM
www.findhornpress.com

CDS AVAILABLE FROM
www.thealchemyofvoice.com

THE ANGELS
OF ATLANTIS

Twelve Mighty Forces
to Transform Your Life Forever

STEWART PEARCE

FINDHORN PRESS

Findhorn Press
One Park Street
Rochester, Vermont 05767
www.findhornpress.com

Findhorn Press is a division of Inner Traditions International

ISBN 978-1-84409-569-8

Cataloging-in-Publication Data for this title is available from the British Library

Printed and bound in the United States

Edited by Michael Hawkins
Cover design by Richard Crookes
Text design and layout by Thierry Bogliolo

Contents

Acknowledgments

Your task is not to seek for love, but to look within and find all the barriers, those that you have built against that love supreme.

– RUMI

Being lost in the forest of life can be disturbing, being found in a meadow of spirituality can be enchanting, yet there is no more profound a virtue in the freedom one uncovers when removing the barriers on the path of the mystical journey.

The sacred Angels who communicate with me provide us with a powerful viaduct to this path and, for this, I thank them with a passion that quickens the core of my heart and soul. For without their teaching, without their wisdom and love, my path and the paths of the many with whom I interact globally would flounder into dullness. To be a vision-holder needs perspective and, by heavens, have the Angels of Atlantis shone a light so bright on my path in moments of challenge. Always there is succour, eternally there is the love that passes all things.

Further gratitude goes to the soul nourishment of the many Alchemediums around the world. These are those who have associated with, and have been fostered by, the initiations of the Temple of Sound Healing known as THE ALCHEMY OF VOICE. Significantly, love goes to Sergio whose amazing technical support, loyal creative drive and hours of loving commitment have enabled me to reach thousands of people with fluency and panache. For Sergio bravely sails the ocean of cyberspace and the further dimensions beyond with great elan.

Peace to Michael for his editorial administrations, the like of which underscore the notion of helping brilliance to shine.

Lastly, profound gratitude must go to my wonderful publishers Thierry and Carol who have provided me with such belief-filled support, throughout the journey of bringing forth these wonderful light-filled Orb-beings of the iridescent Angelic kingdoms.

Namaste.

—Stewart Pearce, London, August 2011

PROLOGUE

Angels as beings of Light transcend every religion, every philosophy, and every creed. Angels have no religion as we know it. Their existence precedes every religious system that has ever existed on Earth.

– ST. THOMAS AQUINAS

Fable upon fable and mystery upon mystery surround the ancient civilization of Atlantis, so much so that many writers have questioned its legendary status. Things that should not have been forgotten were lost – history became legend, legend became myth, and yet a time has come when the Angels will once more help to shape the fortunes of the race of men.

My intention in writing this book is not to create mystique but rather to connect the reader with that part of their psyche that resonates deeply with the notion of Atlantis and the archetypal depth of human nature. For there dwells in most of us a subterranean or subliminal knowledge of this ancient civilization, so much so that people respond passionately whenever or wherever Atlantis is mentioned. You could be anywhere on our planetary domain, from Afghanistan to Zanzibar, and folk become excited at the mention of the name Atlantis; of the great Atla (the Priest Scientists) and how they still may open the archetypes of human experience with their teaching.

My purpose in writing is to illuminate the significance of how the sacred wisdom of Atlantis drenched the human species with the knowledge of drawing spirit into embodiment. How, through a profound reverence for the divine in nature, a powerful bond was created between the celestial and the profane realms of the Universe. Of how the experience of the physical domain on Atlantis allowed the inhabitants to live to a superlative degree, full of joyous union with nature, with an implicit sense of the Cosmos, and in harmony with the other planetary civilizations that permeate the life of Outer Space. All and more became the awareness of those who lived copious Atlantean incarnations, a continent which now lies buried in safe keeping on the ocean floor.

The people of Atlantis experienced a way of being alive that vibrated in accord with a completely different biochemistry from our contemporary molecular status. Their 'super-coherence' was created and nourished by an octave of spiritual intelligence far surpassing anything we currently attain, except perhaps for a few notable exceptions, and it is information about this coherence that I am particularly interested in sharing.

Today, there are a few notable human beings, not unlike the Atlantean Atla Priesthood, who through lifetimes of karmic cleansing have reached a point of rare loving. Who, through years of spiritual quest have sought a point of optimum being-ness, who ,through disciplined service to the Divine, have achieved degrees of enlightenment that vibrate refined states of love within physical embodiment. These beings are the Bodhisattva – 'the living saints' – currently seen in His Holiness the Dalai Lama, the recently departed Sathya Sai Baba, Ammachi the hugging mother, and Mother Meera, to name just a few.

With their light in my consciousness and with instruction from my Angelic guides, a great desire has opened within my heart and soul to write about the Angels of Atlantis, so as to assist with your transformation during this current period of vast planetary and personal change – to create a bridge between Atlantean and post-nuclear man. For, as we look around us at a world that is as volatile as a churning ocean, we may steady ourselves by taking a firm grasp of the eternal maxims of love and joy that lie between the old western mechanistic establishment and the new paradigm of wondrous proportion – the dawning of Aquarius.

As we swim abreast this surge, as we gasp air for another life-affirming breath, as we view safe hope of land, we may see a radically new landscape before us – we may see a paradise where such inner transformation occurs that we are raised to a wholly new level of consciousness, just as we were before when in Atlantis.

Before us lies a vision of ourselves as luminous creative beings, engaged in the evolutionary impulse of the cosmos and, through each passage or step, becoming consciously self-realized divine beings. In this state, we may embody an impulse of love so great that our physical presence will be transfigured, and we will become like orbs of light, transfixed by our energy field.

Behind us lies a rough landscape of challenging definition, strewn with the debris of our growing pains, chaotic in the extreme as we surface from the depths of its shadow, and yet freshly illuminated by the notion of our soul's love – constant, eternal and brimming with unconditional fervour.

Many great minds have written accounts of Atlantis: Plato, Francis Bacon, Helena Blavatsky, Ignatius Donnelly, Rudolf Steiner, Aleister Crowley, Edgar Cayce, and I place myself in humble regard of this vast body of wisdom. Yet, on this occasion, I will interpret a wisdom tradition of divine origin made flesh, which was expressed to me by the supernal guides I have been taught by since the Harmonic Convergence of 1987 –The Angels of Atlantis.

These twelve mighty forces offer a view of the spiritual maxims and archetypal keys that led the Atlantean people to create heaven on earth. These archetypes are keys to unlocking the mystery of our consciousness, to extracting the power of human consciousness from thousands of years of being held within a karmic closet, existing within bands of force that have affected the very matrix from which human intention once sprang.

My meeting with these illustrious Angelic beings, chronicled in the epilogue of my first book *The Alchemy of Voice*, evoked teachings that utterly changed the course of my life and the lives of those with whom I have subsequently worked. For the Angels truly remind us of where the Love Gold lies deep in the very flames of the passion that celebrates the hearth of love – the Heart. For make no mistake, if we open our heart's secret chamber and unpack its love-filled treasure chest, full of the most precious jewels of joy, compassion, empathy, patience, grace, gratitude, freedom, hope and passion, we may truly inherit the joy that is our divine birth-right.

Just as it was in Atlantis, if we embrace the notion of LOVE through continuous moments of our consciousness, that is with a degree of conviction that gestures LOVE IS ALL THERE IS, we blast open the furnace of our spiritual conviction, and the intelligence and compassion of an ancient way of loving sears through our being. Thus a trajectory to heaven is forged.

When the vibration of our soul's note moves us to ecstasy – the unique signature note that is the sonic talisman to this sacred impulse sounded into creation by our heart – we produce a key harmony in human form that stops the symphonic movement of the Cosmos in a second of bated breath. This could be a moment of such exquisite proportion that we would literally hear the voice of the Angels chanting to us, reminding us that our inheritance is to manifest the gifts of grace and truth here on Earth.

For thousands of years, the Atlantean peoples practised cosmic ideals such as these. By chanting and speaking love, peace and abundance into their lives, and because that was all that mattered, they found a way of being full of joy. Sound and its colour-filled resonance, like sparkling light from millions of crystals, connected them to the great jewel of being known as FAITH. Through the acceptance of faith, time and time again, the greatest prize above all was revealed – a sublime connection with the Divine. For this level of spiritual attainment was ordained by the intelligence of the Divine Cosmic Matrix, countenanced by its Angels, governed by the Atla Priesthood, and lived efficaciously by its people.

Today, with the sheer living of this possibility, the Angels inspire us to create intentions for the whole of life that broaden our vistas of consciousness, so that we proclaim bold acts of deep-hearted love through our sacred voice sound fields and use healing modalities such as Voice Alchemy as a transmutational force. These bring pranic upliftment and add vital well-being to the empowerment of our spiritual intelligence. For literally within the core of sound lies the blueprint of creation: of the Cosmos, of the Planet, of your life, and of all sentient life.

Angels of Atlantis

The Angels of Atlantis are:

GABRIEL –	The Divine Messenger
HANAEL –	The Sacred Warrior
JOPHIEL –	The Holy Liberator
METATRON –	The Supernal Teacher
MICHAEL –	The Cosmic Leader
RAPHAEL –	The Holy Healer
RAZIEL –	The Divine Mysteries
SANDALPHON –	The Sacred Guardian
SHAMAEL –	The Divine Guide
URIEL –	The Eternal Companion
ZADKIEL –	The Divine Comforter
ZAPHKIEL –	The Sacred Lover

Atlantis as it was Seen

The vast continent of Atlantis spread across the entire planetary area known today as the Atlantic Ocean – from the Gulf of Mexico in the west, to the area now known as the Atlas Mountains in the east. Although this land mass changed many times throughout the civilization of Atlantis which extended between 250,000 and 11,000 BC, it is during the period between 32,000 BC and 13,000 BC, for just 1,500 of these solar years, that the people lived at a level of vibration far surpassing that we may currently define as healthy, vital, joyous, conscious living.

During this fifteen hundred year period, before the days of completion that moved Atlantis to its watery grave, the Atlanteans lived a supreme Golden Age. This came about because their lives were sustained by a twelve helix DNA, which was so suffused by the light of the Source that they lived lives of blissful joy.

The magnificent bio-chemical symphony of their DNA fostered a physical, emotional, mental and spiritual harmony that vibrated a super-charged status. Life, quickened by this calibration, created a higher frequency super-coherence, within which the people and the planetary life lived in synergy with universal, inter-galactic harmony.

In writing this account, I want to provide a vision of those Atlantean times, when personal mastery as a blueprint of spiritual practice was encouraged by twelve archetypal characteristics taught by the twelve great Angels – for these archetypes are keys to our consciousness, and, as rites of passage, open portals to heaven. Encoded within them are twelve forces that will transform your life forever, brought to you by the co-creativity of the Angels of Atlantis. For co-creation is the Angels fervent wish, in the belief that collaboration, rather than competition, is the next evolutionary step for mankind.

Once we are aligned with the interconnectivity of life's matrix, the condition of we Homo Sapiens (meaning 'intelligence') may evolve to the next level of our incarnation, which might be known as Homo noeticus (meaning 'wisdom'). With this knowledge we will connect intuition with cognition, we will suffuse our heads with our hearts, the rational with the irrational, the conscious with the unconscious, the physical with the spiritual, in preparation for our ultimate state of being Homo luminous, and therefore living as Human Angels.

Angelic Nature

Angels are thoughts of God, and as such have existed in the eternity of the Universe as omniscient, omnipresent, and omnipotent beings forever. Their presence is countenanced by Divine Will to gift humanity with ministrations of Divine Grace. Their role is to love for the sake of love, unconditional and unfettered in its expression. Their work is to vibrate the elixir of grace in miraculous ways so as to re-orientate our perception of this physical plane of existence, the three-dimensional world in which we live.

The Angels light-filled intelligence reminds us of the creative state of immortality that is the only true function of our creative purpose here on Earth. Their love reminds us that deep within each of us is the knowing that we are from the Source, and that to the Source we return when form is resolved, through the fulfillment of our incarnation, the expiation of our karma, and the atonement of our life lessons.

Their presence in our lives provides us with profound keys by which we may evoke a greater wisdom through the expression of our creative purpose through spirit, and that, when this is done to the betterment of cosmic life, as it is written in the great books of Akasha, we return to our origin. This occurs when our soul destiny evolves to that point of Light Emission that calls us from this Planet, and so we return to the Source.

These Angelic beings of light have lovingly looked after us through aeons of time, and yet only assist when we request such of them. Wherever we are, whatever we do, whomever we may be, our Angelic guardians always envelope us in eternal love, harmony and compassion. Except with some human beings, the levels of amnesia developed by the density of our three-dimensionality clouds our perception, and thus we find it difficult to conceive or believe in their supernal wonder.

The Angels teach that Atlantis arose as a cosmic experiment in the northern hemisphere, unlike the civilization of Lemuria or Mu which came forth at the same time in the southern hemisphere. The nature of the 'experiment' was created by an intelligence that existed and still exists in the form of the Intergalactic Federation of Ultra-terrestrial Beings. The council representing the twenty-four civilizations of the Multi-verse is an emanation of Source energy with a consciousness and technology far in advance of current Earth life.

In forming this original creative intention which arose from Source energy, aspects of divine force were expressed in the form of soul groups known as Monads. These arrived from many regions of the cosmos to experience life on Planet Earth, and thence to return the experience to the Source. The Angels of Atlantis suggest that: *at core, humans are sacred beings sent to touch the temporal domain with their creativity, and so they serve as interpreters of the world of matter.*

The Blue Planet

The Angels tell me that the Earth is one of the most beautiful planets existing in the Cosmos. They say that, in the whole Universe, there is no other planet that has the physical possibility of life as here, existing through unique characteristics that form its rare beauty. You see, Planet Earth vibrates through a unique energy field within the Cosmic Matrix, and its physical conditions, created through the fusion of carbon, nitrogen, oxygen and hydrogen, are unlike many of the other planets in the Solar system.

Planet Earth's bio-diversity is so various, so rich, so exquisite that many beings from other worlds have desired physical life on its potent landmass. Having experienced life here, souls want to repeat their incarnation as Terra Firma has a gravitational pull that is different from any other planet and so draws the soul to feel the potential of life within this physical form.

Indeed, the Angels have telepathically suggested that, millions of years ago, the physicality of Planet Earth was entirely that of water, magnetically drawn together by the gravity of two or three celestial moons. Moreover, the molecular formation of H_2O was first brought when the early consciousness of Terra Firma was being formed. For the planet's ultimate destiny was to be covered with water, as a glowing liquid that formed a plane of consciousness, a thought membrane and force that would function as an energy field of super-conductivity. This gave rise to the term the Blue Planet.

Moreover, the purest of energies was to be amplified through the field of the water that covered the planet, just as it occurs through the watery fluids of the human body and, as the water element illustrates in many cultures, the living surface of the planet was to be suffused by a wondrous force – that of feeling. For feeling is the vibrational language of the Source, and therefore feeling is the language of the Soul.

The intention was for an aspect of cosmic consciousness to be made manifest on Earth in a unique way, and so to produce an experience of inter-galactic intelligence resonating with the bio-diversity of Planet Earth and, of all planetary domains within this star system, Earth's biology was created as a bio-diverse paradise to locate this experience.

At that stage of evolution, the decision was made to conduct planetary development through a conscious awareness of feeling. The choice was that Earth would be the only planet of choice, that is, the only planet of free choice in the entire Universe, the only planet for the balancing of the spiritual with the physical, in other words, the creation of a paradise as an unprecedented cosmic experiment.

Thus, the body of water allowed the language of 'feeling' to be conducted. You see, a higher consciousness within the Universe wished to investigate the nature of these energies in three-dimensional form and to advance octaves of consciousness that were hitherto unexpressed. These 'octaves' exist distinct from emotion, as emotions are distortions – they are experiences of separation from the one and only Source – whereas the higher order of feeling is congruent with Divine essence. The Angels posit that Love is not an emotion… it is a higher vibration that brings soul through the various octaves of planetary consciousness.

The Power of Water

Earth's surface water is still 95% salted, and salt water conducts electromagnetic energy with great velocity. Similarly, we know that human beings express their creativity and feeling states through fluid, whether this be through tears, perspiration, joyous sexual exchange, the removal of waste, or the life of the fetus suspended within the amniotic fluid, breathing in and out its life producing juice. Our bodies have always been governed by the elements of earth, water, air, fire and ether.

Water is the super-conductor of feeling – a theme explored by professor Masuro Emoto's work in *Messages in Water* – and as Earth is the only planet of choice, the Blue Planet has become a laboratory for states of contrast that require choice to make them function. These contrasts arise from a binary system that indicates that nothing is singular, for all things are plural. Where there is light, there is dark, where there is thought, there is feeling, where there is love, there is hate, where there is guilt, there is innocence, where there is expression, there is supression, and where there is acceptance there is denial. This list literally moves off into infinity for there are many contrasts that have been created throughout the vistas of consciousness found on Terra Firma.

So we see that Planet Earth has always been pivotal in the evolution of cosmic life, and its closeness to the Sun at the centre of the solar system, shared similarly by Mercury and Venus, further illustrates this. Therefore Planet Earth has become a unique place for each Monad to live, with its three-dimensional vibration frequency, its fascinatingly diverse biology, its binary system of choice, so that the Monads were able to refract into singular formations from their source.

Each soul was given the opportunity to incarnate in a physical body, to experience the sensations of being human by touching the temporal domain. The Angels teach that the human skeleton was formed through a divine blueprint, whilst the muscular-breathing sensory body was created through a spectrum of thought-choice determined by each human being. Each soul became incarnate to possess sole responsibility for its physical form, whilst at the same time remaining in eternal connection with the Source.

Human and Planetary Evolution

We need to awaken a crucial understanding at this time of evolution: that what we need to stretch into is the dawning of a radical new breath. What we need to become aware of is that the choices many of us have made on Planet Earth are not resounding with the highest truth, and therefore our planet is not evolving as fully as it could. These self-exploitative choices have fixed our human condition into the desires of the flesh alone, which constantly grabs for more and more stimulus. Yet, in order for the Universe to evolve, it is quintessential that Planet Earth also evolves. Simultaneously, in order for the other planets to evolve, it is important that we human beings evolve, so that the love of the Universe may generate the energy that feeds the Creator/Creatrix of the Cosmos as one vast in-breath.

Conversely, what has happened on Planet Earth is that many souls have become held or trapped within the atmosphere of the planet, and so these souls reincarnate over and over again in the same world, held in the feverish desire for materialism. This state holds them firmly within planetary force, even though the Earth was originally created to teach the balance between the celestial and the temporal, the spiritual and the physical.

The Angels ask us to see that it is imperative to remove this stuckness in the gravity of the human form. It is crucial that we alert the emotional body to its desires, elevating grosser emotion to a higher plane of pure feeling. It is significant that we remove self from self to create a fulfillment of our energies and, therefore, alleviate the emotional density created by our misuse of gravity.

Then, and only then, may the true reality be revealed – the merging of spirit with body as a manifest purpose of humankind. We must know that within each of us is the key to bring about change; it is our responsibility, our free will, and our choice.

The Societies of Atlantis

The people of Atlantis lived out their earth-borne incarnations through a three-dimensional plane of existence whilst perceiving life from a fifth-dimensional perspective. It was only the Atla Priest-Scientists who were able to access further levels of soul intelligence – from the sixth to the ninth dimension of consciousness and, in some cases, even further. In all, there are twelve dimensions, and the higher levels present a separation from that which we currently perceive as the reality of 3D. These higher harmonic levels move through the tenth, eleventh and twelve dimensions, and eventually suffuse with the Creator-Creatrix principles at the source of creation.

As twelve is the number vibration of universal resonance, the Atlanteans lived in twelve communions across the continent, and the Angels tell me there were 7,000-12,000 beings living in each communion – number seven mirrors the resonance frequency of Planet Earth. The communions were built in circular formations, mirroring the wave energies of the cosmos, which perfected degrees of inclusivity as each individual soul balanced its human choice with that of Divine will.

At the centre of each communion, a Temple was constructed for profound devotion and healing. Living a fifth dimensional frequency meant being in connection with a rare degree of sensitivity – particularly with regard to the holy law of one-ness – and so the Atlanteans attended the Temples for specific rituals throughout the twenty-four hour cycle of day and night. This they did to remain pure within their vibration, by honouring the solar and lunar energies, and in conjunction with the other planetary domains of the Universe.

The rituals were exquisite liturgies experienced through the fullness of consciousness that brings body and spirit together and, in essence, the rituals were interpreted by highly evolved initiates who were ordained as the Atla Priest-Scientists and who knew how to evoke states of mind-altering consciousness, for the Atla possessed the ability to heal with the profound use of Light and Sound.

The vibration of these healing modalities were amplified through the significant use of refined crystals like Diamond, Quartz, Larimar and Amethyst, alongside other semi-precious stones, formed from Planet Earth's geology, or brought from other planetary systems, as there were many visitors from other star systems engaged in the experiment of Terra Firma.

The Crystal Skulls

At the centre of each Temple was placed a Quartz Crystal Skull. These mighty stellar brains, carved from solid pieces of crystal by the use of laser and sonar, were encoded with pure cosmic transmissions from the Matrix.

Altogether, there were twelve Quartz Crystal Skulls and yet, during our current Earth time of 2011, only one has been found, in 1927, during the archeological dig of a Mayan Temple in Belize. This skull is known as the Mitchell-Hedges and, as with the other skulls, it holds powerful cosmic energies that in our current 3D density we have lost the ability to read.

The Angels teach me that the eleven other Quartz Crystal Skulls were dematerialized by the Atla during the end times of Atlantis. You see, the Priests knew all too well the extraordinary power of the Skulls and secreted them within the library of thought held within the etheric body of the great Sphinx at Giza. Interestingly, since the late nineteenth century, geologists have attempted to discover this hall of records, and have been thwarted in their attempts. The reason being that the cache is held within the sound codes of the ancient ones.

The thirteenth skull (13 being the number vibration of spiritual transformation) was made from Amethyst, and resided in the sanctuary of the great Temple of Poseidon. This was the Temple of the Infinite Being, located in an area we now know as the Atlas Mountains of Morocco. Poseidon, the God of the Ocean, was proclaimed the Seal-Keeper of Atlantis – the latter being a sonic glyph for 'the land that rose from the water'.

The Amethyst Crystal Skull was a Gatekeeper Crystal drawing the force of the other twelve skulls into synchrony and creating a portal within the gravity of Planet Earth for the entry of higher-dimensional beings and their information about the life of the Cosmos. The skull was placed within an orichalcum shield beneath the giant Tuaoi Crystal, which was housed within the sanctum sanctorum of Poseidon's Temple. Orichalcum is a golden colored bronze alloy which was used extensively throughout Atlantis for its unique transmission of force.

Indeed, Crystals amplify sonic and light energies, allowing a greater connection with force to take place, for both are pure transmitters of the emanations of Source energy and, as spiritual purity was the key power of Atlantis, these instruments were used constantly to attain healing and sustainable joy.

––––––––––

The Tuaoi, or Great Crystal of Atlantis, was also known as the 'Firestone', and was a cylindrical quartz Star-keeper crystal of vast proportion, cut as a six-sided prism. This was a transmitter for the inter-galactic force that poured through it – solar, lunar, and stellar energies were magnetically drawn to the Tuaoi which, in turn, generated force for the whole continent of Atlantis.

This power generated health-enhanced states for the people, and for the widespread flora and fauna of planetary life. Indeed, the Angels teach me that the technology of the Giant Crystal of Atlantis created an atmospheric dome over the continent, which stabilized the meteorology and promoted a rarefied eco-system. Living within the dome produced enhanced energies for the fifth-dimensional lives of the people, who often lived a span of years far surpassing our present chronology of human life.

The Angels tell me that the twelve Adepts, the highly evolved Priest-Scientists of Atlantis, were the only beings permitted the grace of attending to the Tuaoi and the Amethyst skull. The Priests and Priestesses were extraordinary in their spiritual lineage; arising from the Orion and Sirius star systems, they had passed many soul tests through hundreds of lifetimes of achievement and were profound in their spiritual wisdom and technology. Indeed, they were the harbingers of later civilizations, such as Egypt, the Celtic Nations, Mesopotamia, Greece and the Roman Empire, which I refer to later.

Each of the twelve Angels of Atlantis gave specific service to the twelve adepts, albeit the Angels ubiquitous force meant that they could be present to all beings at all times. Moreover, through archetypal force, they were able to bring planetary, elemental and celestial energies to a point of divine union and, in consequence, this helped the stabilization of the currents of energy that functioned through 3D planetary existence.

The Angel's inter-stellar presence was considered to be profoundly sacred, so much so that the Priests regarded the Angels as celestial guides and sacred attendants. Indeed, this essential belief lived on through ancient Egypt, Greece and Rome, and in *The Egyptian Book of the Dead* there are actually 500 known celestial presences. Whereas, in the antique cultures of the Mediterranean, Angels were made practical in the lives of the people through the notion of the Greek 'daemon' and the Roman 'genius', and were considered the guardian force of each person.

The Atla Priest-Scientists

The Atla Priest-Scientists had seven names, each representing a different aspect of their divine action. These names are protected by astral veils, for if one possesses the name of someone's identity, the person's life force may also be held. Therefore, the Atla' names were only spoken by initiates whose integrity was unquestionable, and they were recorded in the Amethyst Crystal Skull, and to this day are still untraceable. Instead, what exists is how their identities were transmuted into others at the time of the great continental cataclysm.

This was an earth-shaking event, created by the dark force of desire, which completely shifted the magnetic grid of the planet, altering the polar axis. Before this horrific disaster, the Atla telepathically new of the impending doom, and so took the 'ways of truth' to new lands, each supporting the migration of one of the twelve communions. Consequently, this released the dark force as part of the karmic evolution of the planet, and the new land areas became the colonies of the former communions.

The Atla-Priests names became:
AMUN
ANUBIS
HATHOR
ISIS
MAAT
MUTT-NUTT
OSIRIS
PTAH
RA HORUS
SEKHMET-BAST
SETH
THOTH

At the time of completion, the Atla journeyed in twelve specific directions, led by their unique intelligence, and following the Ley-Lines of the planet's matrix, to other powerful earth energy centers. The solar-crystal technology they possessed powered Flying Ships that were used to travel thousands of miles over vast areas of land and water, as well as travelling by the use of mind-altering aspects of their consciousness – for they were Lords and Ladies of weight, space and time. You see, because of their increased intuition and higher levels of psychic intelligence, they could draw on the Cosmic Matrix for energy, and so:

Amun moved to Peru
Anubis moved to Tibet
Hathor moved to the North Mediterranean Islands
Isis moved to Palestine and Ur
Maat moved to the Mayan areas of the Yucatan Peninsula
Mutt-Nutt journeyed to the island now known as Great Britain
Osiris journeyed to Egypt
Ptah moved to Mesopotamia and Egypt
Ra-Horus moved to Greece
Sekhmet-Bast moved to Egypt
Seth moved to what is now North America
Thoth moved to Egypt

The Priest's names in their later Greek/Roman lives became known as:

Amun – Diana or Artemis
Anubis – Poseidon or Neptune
Hathor – Aphrodite or Venus
Isis – Demeter or Ceres
Maat – Hades or Pluto
Mutt-Nutt – Hestia or Vesta
Osiris – Zeus or Jupiter
Ptah – Hera or Juno
Ra-Horus – Apollo or Phoebus
Sekhmet-Bastet – Athena or Minerva
Seth – Ares or Mars
Thoth – Hermes or Mercury

The ideals, archetypes or characteristic vibrations of these beings I will explore in later chapters, and yet look how the number vibration of the Atlantean legacy lives on through the knowledge of contemporary esoteric practice:

1. The 12 Angels of Atlantis
2. The 12 Dimensions of Consciousness
3. The 12 Laws of the Universe
4. The 12 Planets of this Solar System
5. The 12 Astrological Signs
6. The 12 Solar/Lunar Months
7. The 12 Tectonic Plates of Planet Earth
8. The 12 Tribes of Israel
9. The 12 Cranial Nerves
10. The 12 Chakras
11. The 12 Acupuncture Meridians
12. The 12 Apostles of Jesus

Twelve Universal Laws

The Twelve Laws Of The Universe were crucial maxims by which physical life in the three-dimensional nature of Planet Earth was fully comprehended. The laws were considered to be fundamental keys to creation and used effectively to balance the lives of the people. Furthermore, the keys were direct conduits to Source energy and the laws stabilized love, harmony and abundance.

Moreover, by the maintenance of the Twelve Laws, it was believed the divine jewels of unconditional love, patience, charity, compassion, grace, honesty, joy, hope, gratitude, kindness, humility and faith were more easily maintained.

The Laws were:

1. THE LAW OF ONENESS – All molecular energy, of both Human and Planetary force, was considered to be part of the interconnectivity of Universal Consciousness. There was no belief in separation as all things were considered inclusive. Hence the presence of each temple built through the geometry of the circle, suggesting the inclusivity of the feminine principle. Through fifth-dimensionality, the Atlanteans could see the direct effect of the theory of oneness.

2. THE LAW OF VIBRATION – All of creation is composed of vibration occurring in cycles or waves of circular patterning. All outer manifestation was believed to be the vibration of all inner reality. Therefore, the Atlanteans meditated on the vibration of quickening in their lives. They observed the quivering of a leaf in the wind, or the impulse of sound vibrating across water. They truly honoured this powerful force of nature.

3. THE LAW OF RELATIVITY – Each incarnation was chosen to experience initiations or soul tests to strengthen the soul-light within. Each test was seen as a challenge, not a problem, and each individual was taught to remain connected to heart consciousness by loving the natural world. Similarly, it was believed that if unhappiness existed, there was always someone else experiencing a deeper despair. So emotional and spiritual intelligence were taught and experienced as tools for becoming embodied – spirit fully living in matter.

4. THE LAW OF RHYTHM – All of nature vibrates through the rhythms of life, creating the seasons or circadian rhythms, the cycles of nature – such as day follows night through the rhythms of growth or evolution. Positivity was always seen as transformed negativity. Therefore, the Atlanteans honoured the substance of rhythm in their lives by honouring the sacredness of the day moving into night, or of spring into summer.

5. THE LAW OF POLARITY – All parts of planetary force exists through the continuum of contrast – all states exist with an opposite pole. There-

fore, the Atlantean people were taught to change the existence of a challenging circumstance by concentrating on the opposite. Living at a fifth-dimensional level on Planet Earth gave an immediate sense of the difference, and similarity between Earth and the energies of Source. The belief was that no linear reality existed beyond the first three dimensions.

6. THE LAW OF ACTION – All flow exists by being engaged in the action derived from thought, word and deed. Sound brings action to manifestation, so the Atlanteans engaged in sacred voice through song, chant and speaking prayer, to evolve practices of profound action.

7. THE LAW OF ATTRACTION – All thoughts, words and deeds attract like-energy. Therefore, the Atlanteans used the individual, universal and cosmic heart chakras to magnetically draw creation into existence. They saw thought as an electrical force, and feeling as magnetic. They were able to decide on what they wished to attract, and feel what it would be like to have the desired object, all in service to the Source.

8. THE LAW OF MANIFESTATION – The visible effect of our actions may be given in gifts, miracles, blessings and friendship, or as contradictory measures. Therefore, each Atlantean was encouraged to see the daily miracles of life on Earth as a direct consequence of their belief in manifestation.

9. THE LAW OF KARMA – Every action has its cause and effect, its action and reaction. Nothing happens by chance, for what you sow you reap, and when we see life thus, we truly see the grace of spirit moving through all things.

10. THE LAW OF TRANSMUTATION – All beings have the essential ability to transform all conditions so sad becomes happy, and hate becomes love. Applying this universal law through respect of polarity brings powerful healing and transformation through the vibrations of light, colour and sound.

11. THE LAW OF GENDER – All beings and all force have a male and female counterpart. The Atlanteans learned that becoming a Master meant first that you must balance these energies within, and thence become a co-creator with the Source.

12. THE LAW OF INTENTION – All energy flows through intention, and the force that is denied, refused, or resisted, holds negativity rather than supreme acceptance. Therefore, the Atla taught to always focus on the highest ideal, and then the higher levels of spiritual consciousness would be attained.

12 Helix DNA and 2012

With the abiding support of these Laws, the Atlanteans lived with a twelve helix DNA. This state was uniquely refined by the clarity of their intention to increase the light field of each living thing, and was sustained by the twelve chakras of their personal and trans-personal bodies. This fusion of DNA and chakras enabled them to live a fifth-dimensional status and, therefore, their lives vibrated with an increased sensitivity for love and peace. Unified within, this meant an enhanced sense of psyche, of clairsentience, clairaudience and clairvoyance, and these abilities allowed the manifestation of material substance via telekinesis – by mind over matter. These advanced intuitive powers enabled the Atlantean people to easily draw on the force of the Cosmic Matrix, in the same way that the Angels existed.

Similarly, at this time, waves of inter-galactic energy are reaching us from a swiftly evolving Universe and we are being given an opportunity to expand our souls and light bodies to a fifth-dimensional state. As all the planets of our solar system move into a unique axial formation – each planet coherent with the next – Planet Earth will receive an impulse of love from the very centre of the universe so great that the celebrations of December 21st, 2012 will be a festival of love the like of which human beings haven't experienced for twenty-six thousands of years.

Therefore, as the energy matrix of the planet transforms, as the electro-magnetic grid shifts, as the very fabric of our space-time continuum consorts to a different octave, as our light body evolves, we are seeing, and furthermore we will see, extremely unusual global phenomena – the manifestations are limitless. Whether this be through whole-scale seismic activity, dramatic weather conditions, unusual bird and animal behaviour, physiological complaints, rare molecular changes, seasons lengthening or contracting, light enhancing or dissolving, increased UFO or Crop Circle activity, and the immediate manifestation of intended action – all and more will pulse with a new verve and a different tempo. For it is written in the Christian Bible: *If you have faith as a grain of mustard seed, ye shall say unto this mountain: Remove hence to yonder place; and it shall move; and nothing shall be impossible unto you.* (– MATTHEW 17:20)

Guardians of Thought

We must become guardians of our thoughts, for immediate creation will occur whatever the thought as a consequence of the amazing acceleration of planetary force during this time of vast change. Thoughts are things, thoughts bring reality into creation, thought forms create powerful fields of energy that move within us and extend beyond us. They determine our physical and emotional state, for what we think we are.

It is time to resolve the fear-based pollutions, or the repetitive behaviours that have grown from childhood difficulties or from karmic lesions. These emotions fester in the shadow consciousness of our being, bringing myriad challenges. The emotions of fear and anger pollute the rivers of our Chakra system, which is the bio-computer of our whole energy system, and prevent us from opening the trans-personal Chakras of the eighth through to the twelfth. The Chakras enable our light body to evolve and expand – therefore, self-realization is the key – and practicing a different mind-body relationship is the gateway, whilst facilitating the noble rite of the Violet Flame is the solution.

The ancient ritual of the Violet Flame was established in Atlantis, experienced by the ancient Egyptians, re-introduced to us in 1987 on Mount Shasta by St. Germain (the Master Alchemist), and applied by millions of Lightworkers to release, expiate and atone personal or collective karma.

The Keys to Developing Harmonic Mind/Body States

Self-realization arises when we truly recognize:

1. That we are inter-planetary beings from the Source
2. That we are spiritual beings on a human journey
3. That every thought creates reality, and feelings attract outcomes
4. That our biology is our biography
5. That our genetic coding is a karmic choice
6. That suffering occurs when we are not 'consciously living'
7. That meditation brings us into coherence with Source

Practicing Mind-Body states provide us with the knowledge that:

1. Active relaxation through meditation releases toxic stress behaviours.
2. Feelings of love, compassion, joy, forgiveness and generosity ex-

pand the energy field of the body through the health of the heart

3. Daily toning of the body, through cardio-vascular exercise, leads to sustainable health; just as eating and drinking water-based food and fluid substances harmoniously affect our metabolism.

4. Cellular healing through sound and colour leads us to increased light-body emission.

5. Frequent connections with stillness and nature lead us to the master-mistress management of our lives, and our soul's destiny.

6. Living love, empathy and compassion opens our faith to the eternal.

7. Making choices from and loving the Heart brings us into super-coherence.

Facilitating the noble rite of the Violet Flame creates:

1. The expiation of all karma that exists
2. The expansion of our extra-sensory awareness
3. The erasing of the cause behind the effect of disease
4. An experience of one's passion and creativity through the opening of the heart
5. The knowledge of one's position as a force of creation
6. The ecstasy of the interconnectedness of the ALL THAT IS
7. A precise connection with the Source

The 12 Chakras

The Atlanteans lived in a twelve Chakra light body, and these Chakras were wired (through neural pathways) into their twelve-helix DNA. Therefore, they downloaded immunity from the software of the Unified Field of Light into the hardware of their cells through:

12th	STELLAR GATEWAY
11th	SOUL STAR
10th	COSMIC HEART
9th	EARTH STAR
8th	UNIVERSAL HEART
7th	CROWN
6th	THIRD EYE
5th	THROAT
4th	HEART

3rd	SOLAR PLEXUS
2nd	SACRAL
1st	BASE

12 – THE STELLAR GATEWAY

This pure White light force Chakra portal lies several inches above the Eleventh Chakra, at the edge of the light field. Through this Chakra, you may feel your connection with the inter-galactic aspect of your soul's life: it is an energy vortex of vast magnitude through which you may truly experience the cosmic nature of your soul in marriage with the soul of the Cosmos.

It is through this Chakra that evolved spiritual beings, living their spiritual practice as a movement back to wholeness, become at one with the Source. It is an emanation of the Father or Sun aspect of the Christos, the Christ consciousness, and so connects with the apex of your Merkabah. This is the 'chariot' or vehicle for your light body, and it counter-rotates within its geometry as a double formed Star of David, carrying your spiritual and physical body from one dimension to another.

The Atlantean Priest Scientists, the great Atla, used the Merkabah (MER=Light; KA= spirit; BA= physical body) to travel between planetary intelligence, and thence through the use of holograms conveyed the information to the various communions and beyond.

Today, the activation of this Chakra returns us to our original sense of higher consciousness, encompassing the totality of unconditional love.

This Chakra is cared for by METATRON

11 – THE SOUL STAR

This Magenta Chakra connects the soul entity to the feminine aspect of the Christos, represented by Mother Earth, Mary or Quan Yin. Therefore, this light portal lying above the Eighth Chakra gently holds the soul of the human being within the physical body, and is represented by the anointed compassion of the individual incarnation.

Today, we see this supernal energy open within the lives of our leading spiritual wisdom teachers, such as His Holiness the Dalai Lama, the recently departed Sai Baba, Ammachi and Mother Meera. In Atlantis, all living beings were completely aware of their soul star, planetary origin, and reason for incarnating on Planet Earth.

Indeed, the majority of the Atlantean people were from Venus, Sirius and Orion, exploring the nature of being within the physical density of the Earth's gravity.

This Chakra is cared for by SHAMAEL

10 – THE COSMIC HEART

This beautiful Larimar-coloured Chakra lies between the heart and throat Chakra in the physical body, and aligns the soul's incarnation with the interconnectedness of cosmic love, a mixture of heart centeredness and divine expression. It is opened in celebration of its alignment with the consciousness of the twenty-three other civilizations existing in the Universe. These civilizations exist within the far reaches of the Galaxy, and in our contemporary society we are just opening to a responsibility for our extra-terrestrial or ultra-terrestrial neighbours, whereas, the Atlanteans were frequently visited by inter-galactic travelers, thereby opening an expanded awareness of the vast astronomical life existing within the Multi-verse.

This Chakra is cared for by ZADKIEL

9 – THE EARTH STAR

This Gold Chakra lies three to seven inches beneath the feet of the incarnated soul, and allows the notion of Planet Earth's duality to be balanced within the individual. When duality reaches a point of interconnectedness, a comprehension of oneness occurs – the still point of the turning world between the poles.

Furthermore, this Chakra creates a triangular point at the bottom of the Merkabah, and so unifies the upper transpersonal Chakras with the lower personal Chakra. With this intact, Source Energy pours through the individual to restore the harmony of Planet Earth's consciousness. Divine love becomes Earth's loving force and, in contemporary planetary life, we see evidence of this Chakra awakening through people's interest in ecology, the action of co-creation, and the protection of Earth's nature.

Similarly, the Atlanteans lived co-creatively with the Earth Spirits and Mother Nature, and so were extremely alive to the pulsations of Mother Earth within the physical presence of her Sun and Moon cycles, so that her rhythms and pulsations were venerated by all.

This Chakra is cared for by SANDALPHON

8 – THE UNIVERSAL HEART

The Silver of this beautiful Eighth Chakra lies just above the Crown, and its vibratory state connects the individual with the notion of universal love – all living beings are interconnected throughout the Planet and at one within the Universe.

On Earth this Chakra has recently awakened in many people, particularly as a result of the developing attention and concern about the vastly changing nature of our planet's ecology, and the devolution of our establishments. This chakra is the route through which the soul awakens the mental body of the person, illuminating the conviction that "what is above, is also below", and so spiritual discernment occurs on the Earth plane. Objectivity awakens bringing about detachment from conditioned beliefs that are no longer functioning realities within the context of living our lives as spiritual beings on a human journey.

Furthermore, through the UNIVERSAL HEART, we receive oracular messages from the spiritual realms, which download into the seven personal chakras of the physical, emotional and mental bodies.

The Atlanteans ritualized their connection with the universal and earth communities through this chakra, for it was the vector of force that constantly moved them to the conviction of their non-local loving.

This Chakra is cared for by URIEL

7 – CROWN CHAKRA

The Violet of this portal represents the zenith of the seven personal Chakras. Through this energy centre 'light body energy' flows into the trans-personal Chakras of the eighth through to the twelve, thereby linking the nature of our three-dimensional human form with the higher realms of spirit.

The crown Chakra sits a few inches above the top of the head and connects with the pineal gland. This Chakra allows light from the Source to pour into the physical membrane of the individual, and brings connection with the super-conscious mind, the higher self, the cosmic consciousness of God.

This Chakra is cared for by MICHAEL

6 – FOREHEAD CHAKRA

The Indigo nature of this portal is connected with the pituitary gland, and is seen as the 'all seeing eye' of the intuitive aspect of our consciousness. This eye of wisdom looks at the inner seeing of transcendent consciousness, and is awakened as intuition or clairvoyance. Through this 'eye' we develop the ability to see through physical form the underlying energy patterns of the subtle body of the universe.

This Chakra is cared for by RAZIEL

5 – THROAT CHAKRA

This Blue Chakra portal is associated with expression, communication, and the thyroid gland. It is the centre of your higher creative energy and, therefore, creates a transition between your personal will and higher spiritual faith.

This Chakra is cared for by GABRIEL

4 – HEART CHAKRA

This Green Chakra processes unconditional love, empathy, authenticity and compassion. It is connected with the movement between the non-physical and physical senses of self, and is associated with the Thymus Gland.

This Chakra is cared for by RAPHAEL

3 – SOLAR PLEXUS CHAKRA

The Yellow ray of this Chakra is the seat of emotions and will-power. It connects with the Adrenal Glands, and the fight-flight, attraction-repulsion, contraction and expansion impulses which are all triggered by outer stimuli.

This Chakra is cared for by JOPHIEL

2 – SACRAL CHAKRA

The Orange ray of this Chakra portal connects with the issue of polarity, the yin and the yang of the relationship process. It helps us connect and relate with other beings and the world through creative pathways. This energy is associated with the sexual organs and glands.

This Chakra is cared for by ZAPHKIEL

1 – BASE OR ROOT CHAKRA

The Red of this Chakra is the root of the physical body in three dimensions. It focuses our earthly life, and deals with issues associated with survival, endurance, grounding, maintaining and nourishing vital force. It is similarly associated with the sexual organs and glands.

This Chakra is cared for by HANAEL

The twelve Chakras are the bio-computers or databases for the energy field of the human form and, therefore, contribute to the interflowing energy of our four bodies – the physical, emotional, mental and spiritual.

The Chakras are spiritual centres of force, vibrating at a frequency of light seen by those who have the ability to lift their frequency in order to perceive the quality of light that affects the density of the physical body.

For example, in the case of the Eighth Chakra which, when open, formulates a shower of light within the Etheric shield, it can be seen as a Halo around certain beings. View the great paintings of the Renaissance, or Aura Photography, and you will see that a shower of white, silver or coloured light is clearly visible as the God presence of each being.

Cellular Body

At the completion of the Atlantean civilization, much of the inter-stellar force that communicated with the people of the twelve communions began to disconnect its subtle integrations with their lives. This was largely witnessed within the crystal force used to generate power for the communities of people. As the force dwindled, the awareness of the five trans-personal Chakras began to fade, except in certain situations when the Priest Initiates, as highly evolved beings, took their mind-altering practices into special wise enclaves, such as the Ancient Egyptian, the Essene or the Mayan Temples.

As this occurred, each human being's light body began to contract and, in so doing, the whole nature of the molecular force of each person changed. This meant that the remarkable sensitivity of the Atlantean people, and their telekinetic powers, began to diminish – their clairsentient, telepathic, and intuitive propensities literally faded.

Within the light force of the Atlantean cellular body, each molecule shaped into a twelve-helix DNA, and within each helix were thousands and thousands of genes. These genes formulated codes that created each person's nature, and as the light body of each person diminished, so did their DNA structure – moving into the double helix DNA we possess today. However, during the Golden Age of Atlantis, human beings possessed sixty-four combinations of carbon, nitrogen, oxygen and hydrogen – the building blocks of creation – whereas today only twenty combinations exist.

Our work with the Angels of Atlantis is to restore the forty-four remaining codes, to shift our consciousness from the limitations of its current state, and to partake of the supernal joy that is our divine right. For as we heal our physical bodies, we create powerful vectors of force that open our spiritual bodies. Therefore, the pain of loss, isolation and separation begin to disappear, and we return to a total belief in the Source – that space of infinitely unfolding possibility, full of love and joy. As we progress in the direction of bringing heaven onto earth, the temporal challenges of the visible world literally drop away, and we return to a state of bliss.

Significantly, forty-four is the Master number that initiates the meeting point between the material and spiritual domains and, therefore, resonates the purity of Atlantis. If you add together the two fours digits within the number forty-four, the total becomes eight, and if you imagined this digit vertically positioned, you will see the figure of material strength, whereas if you place the digit horizontally it becomes the symbol of infinity – the secret code of divine providence.

Eight-Pointed Star Meditation

Let us use a Sonic Meditation from Atlantis, one that opens the portal of the eight-pointed star, the hidden essence of the Atlantean connection between body and spirit. The Star of Eight is an important number constellation in terms of Earth's stability and balance, and still appears in many cultures such as the eight paths of the Buddha, the eight immortals in the ancient Chinese tradition, and the eight notes of the Octave in the Western traditions – for the sounds of the octave teach all saints to be blissful.

The number eight has universal symbolism, it brings balance, harmony, and cosmic order, and is regarded as a union of the Star's and Humanity's attempt to understand and communicate the unity inherent in all creation.

The eighth planet furthest from the Sun is NEPTUNE, and has a blue hue created largely by the frozen ice that covers its rocky face. As a consequence Neptune is often considered to reflect the surface of the Blue Planet, of the Earth's domain. Neptune or Poseidon was the God of the Sea, and specifically connected with the nature of Atlantis – the name of which means "the land that arose from the sea". Therefore, Poseidon's oceanic domain is associated with the emotional body, and the unconscious mind of humanity.

By using this meditation, we will begin to underpin the nature of the Atlantean experiment in our bodies, we will draw spirit into matter, and make a profound connection with the Divine.

1. Move to your sanctuary (meditation space), burn incense, light a candle, play ambient music to tone the atmosphere, and cradle the intention of love energy around you.

2. Feel your spinal energy aligned, whether you are seated cross-legged or on a chair. Check that you feel grounded, with your feet or sacrum in connection with the ground.

3. Imagine a golden beam of light moving through your spine – this is your pranic cord – down through the strata beneath you until you touch the very core of Mother Earth. Then, once more, bring the golden beam up, up through you, and out through the top of your head beaming off into connection with Neptune. Imagine yourself passing Mars, Jupiter, Saturn, and Uranus to Neptune.

4. Rest for a moment, as you will feel a sensation of this powerful connection reaching deep into your energy field.

5. Then breathe in the very energy of Father Heaven, seeing the light of pranayama moving through the whole of your being as you breathe wide and deep into your physical being. Feel yourself breathing in the blue energy of Neptune.

6. Do this 8 times, aligning your very force with the symbolism of the spirit/flesh connection of Atlantis.

7. Then place your hands on your Heart Chakra, and sound *HAA* three times through your heart, connecting you with your own specific signature note.

8. Then sound *HEE* three times in your Eighth Chakra – this will further draw cosmic energies from Neptune into your being.

9. Then rest for a while, feeling the extraordinary energies moving into your being and into your light body, beginning to fuse a profound connection with the nature of Atlantis.

10. Visualize two deep blue eight-pointed stars covering your heart Chakra, one before and one behind, and spin them in a clock-wise direction whilst you say *RA MA TI MA* three times. Then say *TI RA MA RA* three times. This is an ancient Atlantean Chant meaning: "Everything sacred is blessed – everything blessed is sacred.

11. Then pause, absorbing the powerful energies moving through your heart which is the portal that cradles the divine union between flesh and spirit, the intuitive and cognitive, the material and celestial.

———

This prologue cum chapter rings a clear peal of interesting information concerning life on the continent, and how different the culture, beliefs and mores were from our present societies. Moreover, it sets a backdrop of contrast about living, breathing Atlantis, not in any entirety, but to give a cyclorama of possibilities concerning this extraordinary race of people and how they lived.

The chapters that follow are written as a more lyrical exposition of the twelve Angel's essential characteristics and archetypal values. How they were present in the life of the Atlanteans, and how they are pervasive in our lives today to heal, inspire, provoke, exercise, love and generally aid us with our soul's evolution.

Each chapter contains practical exercises with meditations and prayers, alongside radical information about the Angels' intimate relationship with the Atlantean, Egyptian, Greek and Roman Priests, Priestesses, Gods and Goddesses.

May you feel their presence sanctifying your life!

GABRIEL

DIVINE MESSENGER

"Inspirational messages are blessed strokes of genius."

Aпgel Gabriel

As the supernal Messenger of God, Gabriel brings divine unction directly from the Source – with the sweet zephyr of grace, with the purity of the dove of peace, with the governing boldness of the earth element. Gabriel caresses each of our Chakras with the anointing oil of celestial force.

Touched so, we become blessed in the arousal of our spiritual path, we discover that love and compassion are the only way forward, and our initiation is announced in each breath of Heaven. This divine breathing draws the very essence of the Holy Spirit deep into our beings. It is the conduit for the Angels' progression, and when its mighty wind blows, the essence of 'awakening' lightens our path.

Thence our perception immediately changes, and we are steeped in the fullness of the annunciation which brings divine insight.

The stories of Gabriel are rich and manifold, as we see in the messages to Elizabeth and Mary in the New Testament – they illustrate Archangel Gabriel's ability to create annunciation, to be present at epoch making moments, for both women were explicitly told about their vocation to bring forth sons that would become exceptional beings. As we know, these two sons became John the Baptist and Jesus the Messiah, and indeed they were "great in the sight of the Lord". Fulfilling this sacred role, Gabriel appeared to Jesus shortly before his final hour on the cross, to strengthen the Son of God's conviction with divine aid, and this loving support conveyed Jesus to be 'born into heaven'.

Within all legends of the human birthing process, Gabriel is accredited with the most significant. For Gabriel is the Angel who selects souls from heaven, spending nine months with the unborn child, informing the new life about what he or she will need to know on Earth, including how the soul will be engaged in certain lessons during the forthcoming incarnation, only then to silence the child before birth, by the pressing of an angel's finger on the child's lips, thus producing the cleft below a person's nose.

Gabriel's other legendary tasks involved bringing the Holy Koran to Mohammed, and interpreting the inchoate visions of Daniel in the Old

Testament. For such bounty, Gabriel is considered to evoke the spirit of truth and mercy throughout Islam, Judaism and Christianity.

Gabriel's mighty force illuminates the conviction of the sacred messages we receive from the Divine, and we are always brought back to feeling ourselves closer with God. Gabriel is the governing spirit of the water element – the water of feeling. For we are born of water and, when we accept our soul's transcendent capability, we inevitably feel a movement back to wholeness through the great waters of feeling.

When we enter into the fullness and consciousness of our spiritual journey, we are encouraged through our practice to a greater conviction, and consequently our inner kingdom is edified. When we allow ourselves to feel anointed by the holiness of the instant, we immediately feel touched by the messages of Gabriel's love, and inspiration, delight, and the awe of this evocation drench our bodies.

Gabriel's messages flow bountifully during this year of 2011, for it is a remarkable time of anointing when we are brought to the probability of a rare spiritual alignment, championed by the illumination of the Eighth Chakra – the force of the Universal Heart. This enables the vision of our interconnection with the essence of co-creativity, which moves us to be greater beings of illumination and aligns an increasingly stronger connection with the Divine. For, as we develop maturity as a species, we gain spiritual strength through the many messages of Gabriel.

This is why this great Archangel is known as 'the strength of God' – the supernal message of Gabriel's spirit brings forth the direct content of God's love, awakening the soul, overshadowing one's life with divine luminosity, and pouring light into all actions which shine creativity into existence.

During the 'golden age' of Atlantis, Gabriel's force was likened to a great Oracle and, throughout the ancient world, oracles were thought to be portals through which God spoke directly to man. In this sense, they were different from the Priest-Seers' ability to interpret the signs and metaphors sent by God.

At the centre of the great Temple of the Messenger Communion of Atlantis sat a great Lapis Lazuli stone, surrounded by refined quartz crystals. Lapis enhances oracular wisdom and contains the energies of truth, revelation, loyalty, wisdom, contemplation and communication, and these beautiful crystals together amplified the force of Gabriel's benediction, when placed near the throat and third eye chakras.

Communion of the Messengers

To live in the communion of the Messengers was to be part of a collective who spent their lives aligned with significant aspects of communication, both physical and celestial. Although the Atlanteans didn't use the information technology or tele-communications systems we consider paramount today, instead they used their psychic and intuitive gifts, and through telepathy, teleportation and tele-kinesis created their own specific reality, as a bridge between human and divine, between the planet and the galaxy.

They believed that information moves through the ether, via the ever-present lines of force, similar to that which the Shaman, Wizards and Magicians have used for centuries. Just as our planetary animals migrate by following the electro-magnetic lines of planetary consciousness, so did the Atlanteans, either for sending information between the different communities on Earth, or for determining transmission from the other races of Cosmic Beings. The Atlanteans were always determining their own radar, and in this the planet Mercury played a considerable part as a prime generator. For this reason Mercury was of great significance to the Atlanteans.

Strategy for Connecting with Gabriel

To draw Gabriel and the oracular wisdom of Atlantis closer into your life, to feel the message of this mighty force flowing through your whole body, to hear the whispering of the Angels wisdom in each holy instant, ask questions directly of your higher self – that part of you which moves as the MESSENGER, as a noble communicator.

Speak to the spiritual scribe secreted in the Godliness of your soul, converse with the voice of your love, open your heart to the bounty of its wisdom and, when answers arise, the spiritual elixir of Gabriel will be given opportunity for expression. For Gabriel's voice will always speak with you directly and, when this happens, a loving calm will drench your being, and life will never be the same again.

Ask yourself:

1. Do I have a clear vision of love and joy in my life?
1. Am I full of the conviction of my soul's glory?
2. Can I create greater love and peace in the world?
3. Am I truly compassionate to myself?
4. Is my conduct to other folk full of gracious kindness?

5. Is my sense of self open to receiving divine messages?
6. Has mercy a place in the expression of my heart?
7. Is my life's creativity fully communicated to the world?
8. Do I live the possibility of 'resurrection' in each moment?
9. Am I open to communicating every aspect of my soul?
10. Is my life open to being an oracle in its own right?
11. What messages do I have that bring ultimate truth?

Ponder these questions, venerate Gabriel, and ask this God force to speak with you directly. Listen for the chords of sacred information, trust your intuition, and you will receive direct transmission from this great Messenger, as answers to your heartfelt questions, or indeed any other question that you pose for the intelligence of your soul, just as the Atlanteans did from Mercury.

Atla Priest-Scientist Thoth

In Atlantis, Gabriel administered specifically to one of the twelve great Atla Priest-Scientists, one of whose names was Thoth or Tehuti. When Atlantis came to its time of completion, eventually sinking to its watery grave, Thoth took the communion of the MESSENGERS (the magical speakers, teachers and scribes) to Egypt, whilst the 'diaspora' of the twelve other communions drew them to other parts of the reconstituted Globe.

Great Thoth was known as the "Lord of the Holy Words", or "the Great Scribe Messenger of the Gods". Indeed, ancient Atlantean records suggest that Thoth assisted the creation of the world by the sound of his voice alone, and he was attributed with the inventions of numbering and hieroglyphic lettering. There is no doubt that Thoth was one especial communicator for God.

Just as Thoth's great Atlantean Temple of the Messengers had been encrusted in Lapis Lazuli, so was the Egyptian Temple of Hermopolis Magna. There, Gabriel assisted Thoth's Adepts, each of whom taught the Atlantean system of magic which upheld the powerful elements of creation and which were largely stabilized by the art of Alchemy. The location of the Temple was a hallowed space where the sun god Ra had first become visible and where the rays of the one Light poured onto primordial darkness.

The library of the temple was vast and the sacred books, both in etheric and material form associated with magic, were securely stored in its vault. Part of this stored knowledge was eventually translated during the time of

Hellenistic Egypt, through the works of HERMES TRISMEGISTHUS (the thrice great priest, philosopher and king), and his great book was known as the emerald tablet, or the Kybalion. Although many books were secretly hidden, only the Greek Scholars who emulated Thoth or Hermes translated the few, which, years later, empowered the consciousness of Greek Philosophers such as Pythagoras (569-470 BC), and the great Merlin – a later incarnation of Thoth.

When we absorb the wisdom and practical magic of Gabriel's presence, Thoth/Hermes and Mercury (Mercury was Hermes's Roman counterpart) characteristics emerge within us, and speak through the eons of time. They appear, as if by magic, from the ancient ciphers of the Atlantean library for these idiosyncrasies provide powerful archetypal values to enlighten, heal, enrich and empower our lives.

Make no mistake, these valuable tools can literally emblazon your life with a richer vitality, and are deduced solely from the spiritual dynamo of your soul. You see, these archetypal values are literal keys into the consciousness of your DNA.

The MESSENGERS values for you can be seen thus:

1. The ability to communicate effectively and persuasively
2. An eternally positive attitude towards friendly facilitation
3. A joyous potential for spontaneity
4. Great expertise in public relations
5. Being clear with inner guidance for easy living
6. The ability to be gracious and naturally wise
7. The art of balancing the challenges of life
8. The ability to receive the gifts of life as benedictions
9. The grace to stand as an inspirational witness
10. A tendency to be interested in innovative wisdom
11. A curiosity for the noble adventure of life
12. Seeing that all of life is moved by the magic of Divine Will

Gabriel has innate potential to literally guide our souls to their meaning and message. Therefore, the person who is touched by this Angel's presence is inspired to become centered in soul, seeking access to spiritual truths, and unafraid of venturing into the depths of darkness that can sometimes grip the soul.

Gabriel as Hermes

Hermes guides us from one realm to another with his Caduceus – a rod topped by wings and encircled by two serpents resembling the binary equation of life on Earth – which symbolizes the Male and Female principles entwined, or the swirling spirals of our DNA. The rod as the symbol of the Psychopomp helped Hermes accompany the souls of the dead into the underworld, because Hermes always took the light of the Source with him to lighten the darkness when all else was confounded by the dark.

For example, in the case of Persephone, Hermes escorted her from the kingdom of her dark abduction back to her Mother Demeter. Similarly, Hermes protected Odysseus from the sorceress Circe, who relished dark magic by turning men into swine, and gave Odysseus insight and protection against the Sorceresses power.

Gabriel, like Hermes, seeks to guide the individual with the magic of loving action, opening those who are willing to the meaning and integration of the spiritual realms. Gabriel as a Messenger, like Thoth, employs alchemy to transmute the realm of the earth and its ego, and the collective unconscious or underworld into the magic of pure spirit.

Gabriel as the Healer

In my work as a Voice Alchemist, I have often felt the saving presence of Gabriel, and, like Hermes as the Spirit Mercurius, I've listened to the stories of clients who spoke of their abusive childhoods, or whilst rescuing the inner life confounded by depression, or by hearing about the fortitude of an individual who remained steadfast when lost in the wilderness of the underworld.

For we invite the force of Gabriel in whenever we are truly in need of aid and willing to venture to a new domain. Then we are given the grace of Gabriel to employ an attitude of brave healing, patient emotional intelligence, positive enquiry, benign exploration and wide-eyed curiosity.

When this happens, we actively employ the wisdom and magic of the great Thoth by transmuting the negative into positive, the loss into gain, the guilt into innocence, the hatred into love, the disease into ease. When we call in this archetypal Messenger, we shift the landscape of our consciousness, we radiate with otherworldly might, we expand our soul's longitude and latitude – for the Angel Gabriel is a spark of God's love willing us to experience this degree of ecstasy in cosmic creation.

The archetypal splendour of Gabriel makes the spontaneity of life a unique option between us and the people we meet, the places we visit, the information we receive, and the works we encounter. In this, unusual new happenings are part of Gabriel's magic, often occurring through the charm of synchronicity – those events that appear to be coincidences and yet turn out to be unerringly meaningful. These experiences turn out to be gloriously miraculous and full of uncanny magic.

Living thus, if we harbour a desire to go on vacation or an outing with a sense of adventure, we let the day move within its own fruitfulness, shaping itself by itself. This is when Gabriel is so often with us, inside us, and part of us – loving us, and drowning us in the elixir of the Angels of Atlantis divine unction.

When we celebrate the nature of Gabriel within us thus, when we speak or sing with eloquence and with utter joy, we raise the effervescence of aplomb without a planned script, we respond to life by expressing ourselves with complete authenticity, we play life with the candour and inspiration that resonates deep from within our soul. This is when remarkable charm and generous audacity emerge, electrifying our communications, this is when we liberate our spirit to be a Messenger of the Divine.

AN ANGEL GABRIEL STORY

Roberto worked as a highly talented IT Expert, and was one of my clients several years ago. As soon as we met in consultation, it became clear that there were many reasons for our meeting, not least the fact that Roberto was experiencing acute 'dysphonia' (difficulty in speaking), particularly after spending many hours of concentrated work at his computer screen.

Truth be told, Roberto confessed to being far more at home with the technology of computer science than in establishing harmonious relationships with other human beings, particularly with regard to what he referred to as the 'fair sex'.

I saw Gabriel's beautiful blue hue around Roberto, and I listened sensitively to Roberto's heart-felt plea for liberation from self-doubt and the thwarted desire to seek a mate. So we created a strategy to shift the loneliness and sadness through Alchemy. After which I took Roberto through a journey of understanding concerning the electromagnetic emission of large machines, and how electrical frequency pulsations can displace the subtle biochemistry of the human form. I recommended certain organic shields that could be used, coupled with the powerfully sustaining energy of crystals such as Quartz.

These crystals transduce the electricity waves that can be disharmonious to the body's electrical field. Incidentally, another such practice is to have a cactus or cacti near your computer equipment, as cacti eat the EM emissions.

Secondly, I introduced Roberto to a regime of breath and voice exercises, which commonly allow immediate release from the type of syndrome he experienced. Often when we're mentally concentrating at computer screens, we forget to breathe or indeed only use a shallow breath process through a subtle intake. This closes the throat, tongue root and jaw, so that when we come to vocally express ourselves, we're surprised by the acute tension in our throats and consequent sound. Often, when this occurs, people suggest to me that they do not feel their essence, persona, or soul of sound, which can be extremely disempowering. *Have you ever felt this?*

Roberto left the consultation feeling uplifted, serene and completely aware of what he needed to do and be. Except something strange happened; when he arrived home, he discovered something he least expected – all his computers had malfunctioned, and what lay ahead was much work to rectify the situation. In the middle of this process, he called me expressing a large amount of frustration.

Roberto was open to asking the Angels for a positive resolution to his crisis, and so I recommended that this was a perfect opportunity to ask Angel Gabriel for assistance, particularly as Gabriel governs the Throat Chakra in we humans. Roberto was in agreement, having always felt a close connection with Gabriel through the great stories, and so I created a prayer, instructing Roberto to use it nine times throughout the course of the day. Nine is the destiny number of Gabriel, and the number of completion.

The prayer moved thus:

A PRAYER FOR ANGEL GABRIEL

Dear Archangel Gabriel,
Please fold me in your wings of supernal love and light.
Please hold me in the ray of your Messengers Might.
I pray for loving guidance, oh great one, so that my communication processes, whether they be personal or electronic, be realigned, opened and made free.
I relinquish my will to your power in order to change anything that does not bring forth clarity, love and light in my core nature.

Oh dear Gabriel, please initiate me into your divine guidance and counsel, so that I may meet the expression of my life's partner, and feel able to express my heart's desire.

So be it.

Amen

Forty-eight hours after using this prayer; that is having used it on eighteen separate occasions, all of Roberto's computer equipment was fixed, and more considerably enhanced than before. Two cycles of nine suggests eighteen occasions of prayer (1+8=9).

Through this experience, Gabriel brought divine energies into play, and created a force field of the MESSENGER'S intention. Rather like the emergence of the extraordinary crop circle phenomena, powerful, yet mostly unseen, forces create vectors of goodness and love that bring change to inanimate or animate things.

A daily affirmation to draw Gabriel's force

May I be true to my message
May I be clear in my soul
May I be eloquent in my loving
May I live in ease

Meditation for becoming one with Gabriel's presence

1. Find yourself a sacred space, whether this be in nature, in a consecrated space, or your own meditation room
2. Light a candle, burn Myrrh (Gabriel's scent) and play gentle ambient sound, just to refine the space with the energy of vigilance
3. Feel your spine aligned, whether you sit or lay down – breathe deeply three times, the pranic breath of PEACE, and then be still, forming a Mudra with your thumb and forefinger, by bringing the tips together
4. Feel your whole being open, vigilant and expectant for Gabriel's caress – you may even have a piece of Laps Lazuli that you can hold, or place lightly on your heart or throat Chakra
5. Sense the stillness in the space – this means you are soaking in the great soul field of the Source
6. Breathe deeply and sound Gabriel's heralding sound *EEM* through your heart chakra 7 times

7. Rest – then notice the scintillating air around you, and visualize a beautiful ball of Blue (Lapis Lazuli) Light seven feet in front of you. Notice also a beam of white force shining out from your heart chakra, moving straight ahead of you, and eventually refracting its love currency into this Blue Light of Gabriel. Again, rest and listen to the Oracular whisperings of Gabriel's magical presence full of benediction, grace and inspiration. You will feel the supernal light of the seventh dimensional energies of the Archangelic kingdoms balancing and healing you

Namaste

HANAEL

SACRED WARRIOR

"Courage is the means to shine bravely through love."

TWO

ANGEL HANAEL

In ancient lore, Hanael was attributed with the mystical feat of escorting the Prophet Enoch into Heaven, who then became Metatron. For this, and many other acts of extreme courage, Hanael is called the fire-filled Sacred Warrior and, as such, has a ruby-red force inspired into creation by the planet Mars. This is suitably attributed, for Mars is the red planet in the celestial firmament and, in human life, represents the martial strengths of courage, bravery, boldness and invincibility.

Supremely, Angel Hanael champions force directly from the core of the Source and, as an archetypal force, inspires strength, stamina, steadfastness, purpose and willpower as agents of change, within our lives and the life of the planet. Therefore, Hanael encourages our spiritual muscles to be in peak condition for, make no mistake, we live in a planetary gymnasium for the soul, especially now when we are called to a shifting point of Divine reckoning through the Winter Solstice of 2012.

For this express purpose, Hanael heralds a sense of direction, fostering friendship, integrity and hope, for these are the cardinal virtues of this sacred warrior who emits peace through every breath.

Hanael means the 'glory of the divine', and so this Angel inspires us to fulfill our soul's mission by drawing us to the virtues of honour, faith, trust and love. In consequence, our connection with the Divine is fortified by a special dispensation, and a shield of humility worn by Hanael protects our exquisite hearts. Likewise, Hanael's loving heart reveals that the human heart is the seat of the soul, and so teaches us that, when we open our hearts, we must protect our vulnerability with a shield of humility.

When viewing the beautiful icon that heads this chapter, Hanael's ruby ray feeds us crystalline perseverance and strength, helping us attain powerful objectives whilst shielded by humility. Hanael's motto could be "the main thing, is to keep the main thing, the main thing" – a notion that enables us to concentrate on our devotional pathway when all else appears to fall away. To fortify this, Hanael's force strengthens the red ray of the Base Chakra, from which we express our core identity in the world.

This Chakra energy underlines our separate sense of self on the Earth plane, and brings us to the force of determination that enables a clarification of our soul's journey so that we may release a sense of 'separation' back into the Source. Then the ruby ray of Hanael supplies us with the energy required to identify and cleanse challenge and dissolution, so as to fulfill our Dharma – releasing all illusion and karma as an aspect of Enlightenment.

The Ruby is Hanael's most precious Gem, as this jewel evokes the passion and power of life. As thus, the Ruby was worn as decoration on the body of the great Atla Priest SETH to assist the instillation of passion, courage, perseverance, vitality and leadership. In Sanskrit, the word for ruby means "king of the precious jewels".

Just as we look into the brilliant red rays of the setting sun – 'red sky at night is the warrior's delight' – we may see the boundless sky stretching into the infinity that represents immortality, stretching, as it were, through the expansiveness of our soul's freedom. For freedom is always ours when we stop reducing our sun-filled horizons through the limitations of fear, despair or sadness. This liberation is eternally ours when we meet our spiritual nobility through the sovereignty that claims the eternal as the only reality. For noble actions are the most radiant pages in the biography of our soul's journey.

Here are questions that will help draw Hanael's energy closer to you. This is in order that you feel the force of this Angel's splendour as yours, drawing the ruby force deeper into your whole being and presence:

1. In which situations of my life do I not feel sure and steadfast?
2. What actions in others cause me to feel most vulnerable?
3. When do I feel insecure, and why does this state occur?
4. What aspects do I need to relinquish when feeling fear?
5. Is it difficult for me to concentrate on achieving my life's dream?
6. Where do courage and determination live in my body?
7. What do I feel about defenceless action in the face of aggression?
8. How can I become the Captain of my soul?
9. Are there skills I could learn to increase my perseverance?
10. Have I released negativity from my being, such as defensive anger?
11. Do I react, or do I respond, to life's challenges?
12. Are there any situations in my life that stifle my passion, and how can I cleanse them?

These questions, and others like them, will bring you to a point of reckoning your soul's content, and this alone will allow you to release untruth or illusion back into the Source, through Hanael's might and guidance. This is the major reason why the Angels come to us at this time of spiritual evolution, for they wish to support us with an unwavering love whilst we search for truth, by taking our lesions from us.

Being a sacred warrior means that Hanael cuts through any of the contempt you bear for yourself, for your life, for other human beings, for situations or buildings, for any of the myriad forms that do not permit you to glory in the divine that lives within you. So, if you feel you need help to resolve any of these challenges, please consult someone whom you feel you can trust. Perhaps this will be a Therapist or Counsellor who has the warrior's zeal and who can provide you with profound strategies to cut through the canker in your emotional body. When completed, this means you will shine the true might of the archetypal warrior that lives inside you, resplendent, glorious and utterly authentic.

The Atla-Priest Scientist Seth

During the life of Atlantis, the Atla-Priest SETH governed the communion of the Peaceful Warriors, guiding and instructing the energies of disharmony into harmony, thus aligning those energies that were untamed in human nature and that brought forth fear.

Interestingly, Seth was also given responsibility for directing the weather conditions of Atlantis, so that inclement weather could be brought back to peaceful sunshine. Indeed, it was the Priest Seth who inspired the creation of a gigantic biosphere over the entire continent of Atlantis. This dome shaped plane of force refined the climate of the continent, enabling an edifying atmosphere to exist which sustained a level of spiritual attainment that vibrated on a high octave. If biological energy wasn't in coherence with this force, it was immediately transmuted, and so the Atlantean people developed an enormous power within their spiritual technology concerning the Divine being made manifest in human form.

This evolutionary process created the development of new thought-forms, new beliefs, new relationships and new patterns of behavior, and with each of these forces there was the potential to bring forth chaos as well as order. In relation to this, the High Priest Seth taught the creative nature of conflict, and how fraught force can always be relinquished into the safe keeping of the Divine. The rituals he initiated were based on the purification of conflicting Mars energy.

Set gave particular attention to the development of physical power, emphasizing this prowess as a means for the spontaneity of creative action.

After thousand of years of instilling noble action in the Sacred Warrior communion, during the end times of the Atlantean civilization, Seth took the Communion of the Warriors to Japan. There he founded a nation of sacred warriors, which we have come to know as the famous Samurai. From the earliest times, the Samurai lived the path of the warrior as a way of honour, emphasizing duty, allegiance, courage, bravery and loyalty as core life disciplines.

Later in the Greek civilization, Seth took on the form of Ares, and in Rome, Mars. Ares was the Greek God of War, and Mars was the Roman God of Protection. For the Romans, Mars was seen as the father of Romulus and Remus, the twins who founded the great city of Rome. Whereas in the stories of Greece, Ares fell in love with Aphrodite, the Goddess of Love, with whom he sired three children – two sons, Deimos (Fear) and Phobos (Panic), and a daughter Harmonia, representing the virtue of Harmony.

The Archetype of the Warrior within Human Nature

Linking with the archetype of the warrior through Hanael's inspiration means we begin to embody the characteristics that may embolden our spiritual pathway with excellence and purity. Embodying Hanael energy means we become assertive, impulsive, active, intensely emotional, and alive within the motion of our bodies. Processing the sacred creativity of the Angelic order thus means that we exorcise the shadow complex of a God of War, who reaps negative behavioural traits. Becoming the shadow side of warrior force means that one becomes overly impulsive, prone to angry reaction, a philanderer or exploiter of opinions – garnering interest in only that which billows out one's ego. Whereas the light-filled character options of the warrior bring us to a point of valiance that sustains our spiritual path with uncompromising valorous truth.

The WARRIOR's positive values may be seen as:

1. The ability to lead and create ideas in any given situation, particularly when one is tested
2. An inspirational propensity to respond to challenge as an opportunity for growth
3. A joyous regard for the gift of spontaneity
4. Expertise in solving problems from an emotional perspective, and therefore transmuting all negativity whilst holding the glory of emotional intelligence in the highest regard

5. A healthy attitude for the energy of playfulness, ease and flow
6. The ability to remain steadfast and loyal to a person, organization, or a value of excellence
7. The art of willing change to occur
8. The ability to see life as a joyful adventure
9. The quality of mental and emotional flexibility in all creative situations
10. The ability to be immediate and loving in all situations, without worry
11. A believer in the substance of will-power as a leading determinant for the success of life as a project of love and truth.
12. Seeing that all of life is moved by the magic of Divine Will

The ancient stories of Ares show the shadow side of the Warrior. For example, in Homer's *Iliad*, he is seen as bloodthirsty, contemptible, revengeful and a whining liar. Ares is perceived as being hot-headed, whinge-hearted, and repeatedly shamed by his sister Athena. He is described as one who knows no right, one who is constantly over-reacting through irrational emotional behaviour, one whose feelings are intemperate and indulgent, and one who is motivated solely by retaliation and spite.

In another story, Athena guides Diomedes to wound Ares with a spear, and so Ares retorts, complaining to Zeus. Whereupon the great King God merely rejects and humiliates him further, by suggesting that Ares is the most hated God on Mount Olympus.

These accounts are pretty dark, and may have sprung from Seth's involvement in the catastrophe of the Atlantean end times. Interestingly, the Angels won't reveal to me the Priest-Scientists who were directly involved in this act of violence, suggesting that, if names are revealed, their presence is evoked and as there is still much Atlantean karma to be expiated, the Angels prefer to let the matter rest.

The Atla each bore twelve names, consisting of layers of vibration that revealed different characteristics of their humanity, through to their Divinity. Each of the one hundred and forty-four names is recorded in the Amethyst Crystal, which once was resident in the great Temple of Poseidon, and at a time when the information can be revealed, we will receive their attribution and meaning.

Let us move to Hanael's unique vibration:

An Angel Hanael Story

Henry was an experienced Finance Broker and Hedge Fund Manager who became a client of mine as a consequence of suffering from a duodenal ulcer. The symptoms were aggressive heartburn, gnawing pains in his stomach, a burning sensation in his throat, and a feeling of complete fatigue, all of which led to a major loss of energy and a crippling feeling of disorientation.

Henry's condition was very serious, and so he and I worked in association with his allopathic physicians who had prescribed acid-suppressing drugs, and as Henry's predicament was severe, he vowed allegiance to the Doctors' drugs. I suggested extensive relaxation processes including deep breath and sound work to ease the symptoms and to release the associated tension so that Henry could begin a journey towards understanding the cause.

Henry felt his debilitating physiology had been initially challenged at the Royal Military Academy Sandhurst where he had trained as Army Personnel, a role that had become exacerbated by spending time in Afghanistan. Time in active service had led to depression, and so Henry had quit the Army, feeling himself drawn to peace rather than existing within the constant horrors he had experienced during active combat.

Henry's emotional state led me to understand that he was archetypically composed more of the peaceful warrior than of the 'fighting machine'. Henry's soul belief harboured the release of injustice and the creation of harmony rather than the cut and thrust he had experienced in active service. I suggested we also bring in Hanael's aid for steadfast healing and creative inspiration.

I recommended Henry use this prayer:

A prayer for Angel Hanael

Dear Archangel Hanael,

Please bring me comfort as your willing servant.

Please bring relief to my physical condition, and fill my contrite emotional body with healing, so that any anger may be resolved and sent back into the Source.

Please assist me with your Warrior's strength, and enlighten my path when I stray from certainty.

Please enchant me with the verve of positivism and joy, so that I may find my rightful path as a bringer of Peace and Love.

Please show me the clarity of my destiny, and prevent me wavering from my soul's path.

So be it.

Amen

Henry's physical state became easier through the use of this prayerful meditation, so much so that he felt assured about moving away from the drug-therapy prescribed by his doctors, replacing these procedures with a specific health regime recommended by a favoured Homeopathic Nutritionist. Henry also adopted the Sonic Meditations I recommended.

On several occasions during meditation, he noticed a change of temperature in the room and saw a beautiful red Orb circling his head. What other confirmation could he wish for, knowing that Hanael was working closely with him! Therefore Henry felt aided to redirect his whole being through the steadfast promotion of vitality and health and, in consequence, summoned a courage and steadfastness that helped him make a complete change of profession.

Six months later, this was still the case, as Henry felt Hanael's energy drawing him forward, helping him through a major career opportunity working for one of the UK's leading charities. To this day, Henry's life is completely transformed, full of joyous wellbeing, and he is happily married to a beautiful woman who sports an exquisite ruby ring as her wedding present.

A DAILY AFFIRMATION TO DRAW HANAEL'S FORCE

May I be strong
May I be courageous
May I be steadfast
May I live in peace

MEDITATION FOR BECOMING ONE WITH HANAEL'S PRESENCE

1. Find yourself in a sacred space, whether this be in a natural landscape, or your meditation room

2. Light a candle, burn some Geranium essence (Haniel's scent), and play ambient music to prepare for Haniel's presence

3. Having consecrated the space, breathe out the intention to be gratified by the presence of Hanael, and if you can, hold a piece of Ruby in your hand or place it on your heart Chakra

4. Align your spine, create a Mudra by placing your thumb and forefinger together, and feel your whole presence vigilant to the space, whether you are sitting or lying down

5. Breathe deeply, with the breath-light moving through your whole force, and feel SILENCE, SOLITUDE & STILLNESS moving through you – the latter will utterly nourish your soul

6. Breathe deeply and sound *OM* through your heart chakra 7 times. This will draw Hanael into your energy field

7. Rest and notice how pure force extends from your heart into the space by seven feet. As your force intensifies imagine a beautiful Ruby Ray Orb Light emerging at its apex; this is the force of Angel Hanael. Listen to the Oracular whisperings of Hanael's magical presence full of courage, hope and willpower. You will feel the supernal light of the seventh dimensional energies of the Archangelic kingdoms integrating and healing you

Namaste

"Liberation is the call of the soul to action."

THREE

Angel Jophiel

Jophiel arises from the Atlantean ether as a beautiful Yellow Orb. This Angel is as hallowed as the story of creation itself, and gathers life on Earth as a liberating agency. Jophiel's distinct signature is written in the power of the beautiful Citrine Crystal.

Indeed, there exists an ancient legend which tells of Jophiel giving the Earth its Citrine mineral during the liberation of Adam and Eve from the protection of the Garden of Eden. Once divine knowledge had been embodied in Adam, Eve and the life of the garden, time decreed that the essence of this time should ascend to other levels of being, and so Jophiel gave us the beauty of the Citrine to use as a 'calling stone' for the force of liberation.

Citrine is a gatekeeper for drawing in the presence of powerful celestial forces. It is the essence of freedom itself incarnate, just like the profound teachings of Gautama Buddha, who taught us to find detached bliss from the darker aspects of our emotions that we so often give our power to. Meditate on the beautiful icon that heads this chapter, and you will further absorb the force of detachment and liberation.

Yellow as a tonal colour, refracted from the 'great light', is the third rainbow ray of the visible spectrum and, in human life, vibrates to condition the third Chakra of the Solar Plexus. This is the portal for the liberation of our physical will and, as such, is as ancient as the winds and stone. This energy centre pledges allegiance to the Crown Chakra so that a point of transcendence may be created. Therefore, this bridge draws all profane emotion into divine detachment, and so to liberation. Therefore, this Chakra governs the vectors of will, both through gain and loss.

During the days of Atlantis, Jophiel was considered to be the Archangel of the Wise, for in Jophiel's presence one could attain the wisdom of connection with one's higher self. Like the theme of Jacob's dream, liberation through Jophiel's force can be seen as a cosmic ladder.

For, as we climb in the company of this supernal being, we are taken into the halls of the all-knowing ones – the Ascended Masters and Angels, who live in the higher dimensions and lead us to greater communion with the Source.

Likewise, the sunshine ray of Jophiel's energy is brought to us each day as a means to create fresh approaches regarding every aspect of life. Like the beautiful Sun Flower, we are returned to the thrill, delight and sheer pleasure of how enchanting life is, and if we sun-gaze into the yellow/gold ray, we become at one with the sun of the Source.

The planet Saturn from which Jophiel draws so much energy governs the galactic energy that manifests the law of Liberation. The law of manifestation denotes what we want in the world, and Saturn has the ability to help us focus, concentrate and work out our karma. Saturn indicates what work we have to do to become 'lighter', and therefore to liberate ourselves from the cycle of repeated lives that occur, until we receive the message and expiate the actions of the past. In this special regard, Saturn interrelates and serves the great Jophiel with its beautiful yellow rays, created largely by its hydrogen-helium surface.

If for some reason your life doesn't appear rich, if your creativity feels moribund, your self-esteem low, your mental body unclear, or your physical body bound by tension, ask Jophiel to bring the essence of liberation to you. Then, your force, your Saturn force, will realign, and automatically your hope will be restored – for hope springs from the place of eternity, like a flame of wisdom enlightening, discerning, illuminating – making all things clearer so that the mind is once more free.

I've found over the years that Jophiel brings such an 'awakening' charge whenever one needs this degree of stimulation. So if you ever feel a lack of joie de vivre, when your spirits are dulled by challenging news, when you are met with the deafening noise of worldly corruption, when you feel pinched by the rawness of life at the edge, or when the spectre of sorrow visits you, draw the Yellow Ray of Jophiel's energy around you, gaze into the deep beauty of the Citrine ray, and your mood will automatically change.

Jophiel brings vitality, stimulation, and the power to liberate one self from the prison of negativity or from the slough of despond.

To draw Jophiel's energy closer to you, to feel the force of this Angel's splendour in the flesh of your being, answer the following questions:

1. In which situations of your life do you not feel liberated?
2. Which activities bring you to feel greater liberation is needed?
3. What do you need to do to regenerate your being?

4. In which aspects of yourself do you need to expand your creativity?
5. What health regimes best support you?
6. Where in your body do you feel detachment from negative impulse?
7. Which aspect of your emotional life needs optimum healing?
8. How can you bring a greater sense of liberation to those you work with?
9. Which parts of you do you need to unify further with God?
10. What liberations can you bring to your brothers' and sisters' lives?
11. Is life a constant temple for the joy of wellbeing?
12. Are there any situations in your life that need to be expiated?

Ponder these questions, and venerate Jophiel as a God-force speaking with you, then hear the chords of sacred information. Trust your intuition, and you will receive direct transmission from this great Liberator in the form of answers to your heartfelt questions, or indeed any other question that you pose for the intelligence of your soul.

Communion of the Liberators

In Atlantis, Jophiel served the communion of the LIBERATORS, and the great Atla Priest-scientist PTAH. This sacred community dedicated their lives to connecting the energies of the Divine Matrix with the Planetary Matrix. Their roles were multidimensional and suffused by the notion of being at the forefront of creation, for Ptah was one of the major influences that beheld Planet Earth's energy as a cosmic experiment where the divine could be recreated in physical form.

During the end times of Atlantis, Ptah led the communion of the LIBERATORS to Mesopotamia – the area of land between the Tigress and Euphrates, known today as the 'fertile crescent'. There they formed the astounding Sumerian civilization that helped to shape much of what we know of the Babylonian and Assyrian Empires.

In Egypt, and at approximately the same time, Ptah was considered the Father of all beginnings, and a living vortex of the great Creator. Ptah was depicted holding the four elements of earth, water, air and fire as reins, and as such, this Priest-Magi was the Lord of regeneration and life, for these elements correspond with the building blocks of creation – carbon, nitrogen, oxygen and hydrogen.

Atla Priest-Scientist Ptah

Ptah's Temple in ancient Egypt was at Memphis, a city designed as the political centre of Egypt. Temple rituals and dedications were designed to harness cosmic power made manifest on Earth, just as they had been dedicated to LIBERATION in the great Temple of Atlantis. There, Citrine, Quartz and Golden Beryl were encrusted on the walls and floors, producing extraordinary yellow rays to enhance the grounding of divine potential. Harnessing this force brought physical progress and material success, utilized in order to alter the life of the whole community. Just as then, so it is for us now – when true power is made sovereign, our physical, mental and emotional bodies are aligned with our spiritual essence, and once again Ptah holds our lives in the reins of his power.

Ptah appears in an interesting form through the Greek civilization. There he was seen as the Goddess Persephone (Proserpina for the Romans) appearing as the Queenly liberating guide of the underworld (the shadow), and reigning over dead souls whilst assisting the living.

Characters like Heracles (Hercules for the Romans) visited the underworld for archetypal cures, such as the completion of his twelve 'labours', the tenth feat of which was to leash the three-headed guard dog of the Underworld (the three heads represent desire, sensation and intention) known as Cerberus. Yet, before doing this, he was guided to crave permission from Persephone, who granted it willingly. Painted thus, Ptah and Persephone hold different sides of the same coin: one as the liberating King of the over-world, and the other with similar influence, but this time as Queen of the under-world.

The LIBERATORS positive values may be seen as:

1. The ability to liberate the soul from the confines of imprisoned thought or feeling
2. A propensity to forgive and let go of old patterns
3. A joyous ability to seek the positive in life's challenges
4. An instinct for the energy of protection over the vulnerable
5. A detailed awareness of how negative can be offset by positive
6. The will to detach from compromising emotionality
7. A caring regard for transmuting flesh crises into spirit gains
8. The fun of playful encounters
9. A profound recognition of spiritual practice
10. The awe of spiritual discernment

11.   A believer in the faith of human conduct as transcendent
12.   Seeing that all of life is moved by the magic of Divine Will

An Angel Jophiel Story

Several years ago, I was presented with an extraordinary story about a political journalist from Chile, who had been captured and cruelly treated during a period of imprisonment. This all took place during a time of excessive civil unrest and military dictatorship.

During her incarceration, Maria had been horrendously tortured, and on one occasion had lost her voice completely for at least one month during the three years of captivity. Although her recovery was seemingly complete, Maria was still keen on gaining a greater comprehension of the period she had spent voiceless, and yet, on meeting her, I was aware of how centered her voice was – it had great flexibility and easy tempo. In truth, our initial encounter was surprising, because instead of meeting the victim of the harrowing experience I had heard about, there stood before me a beautiful being of benign and gracious countenance, smiling with effortless ease, and showing no visible scars of the horrific turmoil she has withstood.

During our conversation, an extraordinary story emerged: whilst imprisoned and experiencing the most intense period of cruelty, Maria had also experienced persistent and acute out-of-body states. These episodes had been preceded by concussion, when she had lost consciousness for only a short time and then, on waking, Maria came to sense a bright yellow light around her. Initially dazzled, it took only a few moments to realize that the light was also accompanied by a high-pitched harmonic, centered within the colored Orb of yellow light, several metres above her head.

It was then that she became aware of her 'voice loss', and as she attempted to express the enormity of what she experienced, it seemed that her voice had been literally taken from her and somehow replaced by the harmonic tones emerging from the bright yellow light. In these moments, a vast conduction of energy drenched her being, she felt wrapped in LOVE, and heard words of a language she couldn't comprehend but which seemed ancient and Elvish, as though derived from the earth, wind and water of the natural world. This encounter finished as a palpable wind moved through her prison, which was completed by several moments of grave stillness that completely confounded her captors.

From that moment onwards, she had felt a serene inner calm and connection with God, and simply knew that, even if her captors continued beating her, they couldn't access that especially crucial part of her, her soul-filled empathetic truth.

It was a fervent belief in loving truth and social justice that had drawn her to journalism in the first place, and Maria wished her media profile could be used as a medium for exposing the desecration of human rights that had taken place in her country during its period of dictatorship. Maria wished to nullify or exorcise the mark such cruelty had made on her fellow citizens' lives.

I was fascinated by this story and became aware of the exquisite presence of Jophiel's energy around her, for flickering yellow/golden lights surrounded her in waves of force, which instructed me in the belief that her voice loss wasn't a loss at all, but rather a gain of another quality of sound, that being a gift directly from the Source. This had been metered down through the various octaves of energy that make up our planetary matrix. Furthermore, these changes of dimensional force create altered states of behaviour in us, and so our physiology appears to change to accommodate the force, often in surprising ways, and thence we are utterly changed by the miracle.

The undeniable fact was that Maria's imprisonment, and her subsequent life had been radically changed by the Angelic encounter. We gloried together as I chanted Jophiel's presence into her awareness, and Maria felt so liberated by the yellow light and sound of the sun-drenched love that filled her. Thenceforward, she was able to sing her own song of freedom through the peace work she was destined to carry out.

I suggested that Maria use this prayer to enhance her connection with Jophiel:

A prayer for Angel Jophiel

Dear Archangel Jophiel,
Thank you for your wings of bright light beating liberation into my day and nights.
Thank you for protecting me during those times of ultimate challenge.
Please bring clarity to my peace work, filling it with divine grace.
Please assist me in the deeper release of my karma, and enable me to burn steadily with forgiveness, as I love the souls of those who tormented me.
Please allow me to find greater peace in meditation so that I feel the joy of the Source through each and every breath.
Please share with me opportunities for pure joy so that, as I walk the path of life, I may shine a radiance that inspires other to their liberation, in full belief of their soul.
So be it.
Amen

A daily affirmation to draw Jophiel force

May I be liberated
May I be forgiving
May I be full of joy
May I live in peace

Meditation for becoming one with Jophiel's presence

1. Place yourself in a sacred space, whether this be a natural landscape, or your meditation room
2. Light a candle, burn some Narcissus essence (Jophiel's scent), and play ambient music to prepare for this angelic presence, and to consecrate the space with a pure intention
3. Having consecrated the space, breathe your intention to be in the presence of Jophiel throughout the space and, if you possess a piece of Citrine, hold it in your hand or, if lying down, place it on your heart Chakra
4. Align your spine, create a Mudra by placing your thumb and forefinger together, and feel your whole presence vigilant whether you are sitting or lying down
5. Breathe deeply with the breath-light moving through your

whole being. Feel SILENCE, SOLITUDE AND STILLNESS – the latter will nourish your soul

6. Breathe deeply and sound *OM* through your heart chakra seven times; this will draw Jophiel's presence into your energy field

7. Rest and notice how pure force extends from your heart into the space before you, by seven feet (2m). As your force intensifies, imagine a beautiful CITRINE Orb of light emerging from the end point, the Saturn force of Jophiel's love. Then rest and listen to the Oracular whisperings of Jophiel's magical presence full of courage, hope and willpower. You will feel the supernal light of the seventh dimensional energies of the Archangelic kingdoms liberating and healing you

Namaste

"Where there is passion, there is purpose."

FOUR

Angel Metatron

From ancient times, a belief has existed that the brilliant white Diamond light of Metatron is the most rare – beyond compare. Things that were, things that are, and some things that have not yet come to pass, are the energies that vibrate through the Diamond Ray intelligence of mighty Metatron. For Metatron's force overshadows the most ardent spiritual being in their quest for enlightenment – the great search for the essence and reflection of life's love and freedom.

Metatron is one such reflection, emerging from the Source as a thought of the Divine, and enlivened in the Old Testament as the Prophet Enoch. Interestingly Enoch, alongside Elijah, are the only men recorded in the Bible to have been taken directly to heaven by God in recognition of their unparalleled purity whilst on Earth.

In another Old Testament story, Abraham is discovered about to sacrifice his only son Isaac as a sign of his obedience to God, and it is Metatron, as the very instrument of God, that commands Abraham to cease perpetrating the act. Subsequently, Abraham's obedience and humility to God is magnificent.

Then, in another story, as Moses ascends Mount Sinai, wishing to see the face of God, he instead meets the burning bush, and so feels the pulsing light of Metatron, for it is this great Angel that appears as the very glory of nature when summoned by the Divine.

Metatron is the Angel of the sacred presence, sitting on the right of the Divine and, as such, hears all mediations and all meditations. This lofty function has developed for Metatron through the sands of time, for Metatron is the supernal teacher who holds the key to the Akashic records, the great book of all thought. This attribute is recorded in the icon above, as we see Metatron dispensing divine knowledge whenever the request is made.

Metatron, as the white ray of purity, is comprised of, and reflects, all others, including the supernal colors of the higher octaves that exist beyond human perception. Therefore, Metatron may be evoked by concentrating on the beautiful Diamond Ray in the icon above, and you will be brought unprecedented spiritual growth, for Metatron is the major dial of Angelic consciousness that calibrates divine and human forces on Planet Earth.

Angel Metatron champions the STELLA GATEWAY Chakra, the chakra that contains all the information of your soul's code and the many incarnations you have lived. When vibrating fully, this trans-personal chakra, existing at the edge of your energy field, activates your Merkabah, and your light body awakens to truly begin your ascension as a cosmological being.

Communion of the Teachers

On Atlantis, Metatron served the communion of the TEACHERS and spoke through the great Atla AMUN, the Priest–scientist that led the community with an unparalleled loving countenance, for within the Temple of the Teachers were some of the most powerful Quartz crystals existing in Atlantis. These were called 'Star-Markers', they were housed in a beautiful Diamond Shrine and, when fully activated, brought transmissions from the ancient records of the matrix. These refined teachings led the Atlanteans forward through the sands of time.

In alignment with the Star Marker crystals, the TEACHERS of Atlantis took the role of Oracles, allowing the many messages of knowledge to flow through their communications which were deduced from the great records of original thought within the Akasha. All learning was considered to be remembering, and the teaching templates used were many, involving sacred art, music, drama and dance. All templates were designed to experientially aid the opening of fields of human consciousness.

As all Atlantean people lived a twelve helix DNA, adopting beliefs and lifestyles that endorsed their connection between the human and divine, so many of the skills taught brought the children to an accomplished understanding of their telekinetic and telepathic psychic abilities. Indeed, temple rituals led each person to understand how purity, innocence and grace would create such harmonic resonance, such coherence, that individual creativity would abound freely, enabling a greater connection with the Planetary and Cosmic Matrix.

Therefore, teleportation, levitation, the manifestation of material abundance, the creation of beautiful architecture through the laser power of light and sound, healing through psychic surgery, the production of coherent resonances through meditation, chant and prayer – all and more were the daily practice of the Teachers and students in the great Temple of Divine Intelligence.

Speak to the spiritual teacher secreted in the Godliness of your soul, converse with the voice of your love, open your heart to the bounty of its wisdom and, when answers arise from the very centre of your soul, the celestial elixir of Metatron will be given opportunity for expression. Then, Metatron's voice will speak with you directly, loving calm will drench your being, and life will never be the same again.

As you draw Metatron's energy closer to yourself, as you awaken through the pulse of this great Angels force, as you feel the great impulse of extra-sensory vibration moving through your own behaviour, ask yourself how you may enliven and enrich these states through the following questions:

1. Are you clear about the profound teachings of your life?
2. Are you sustained by the conviction that each moment of life is miraculous?
3. Does your love flow with mercy in response to the world?
4. Do you honour and celebrate your wise soul?
5. Is your conduct to other folk full of graciousness?
6. Is your sense of self open to receiving divine messages?
7. Do you allow yourself to truly record divine intelligence in your life?
8. Is your psychic creativity fully communicated in your life within the world?
9. Do you live the probability of your creativity pulsing with light?
10. Are you open to the teaching of your third eye?
11. Is your life open to oracular information?
12. Do you know that life utters itself through words of integrity?

Ponder these questions, and celebrate Metatron as the God force within you. Hear the chords of sacred information directly communicate to you from the great Akasha. Trust your psyche and, using your heart as a dowsing instrument, you will receive direct transmission from this supernal Teacher about any point of life you personally need help with.

These teachings will fill your life and soul with such awe and joy that you will desire to further your connection with Metatron's force time and time again, just as you did during your lives in Atlantis.

Metatron's force is especially linked with Planet Earth, its destiny and its people and, unlike the other Angels of Atlantis, is not attributed to other planetary responsibilities (such as Gabriel with Neptune, Haniel with Mars, or Jophiel with Saturn, for example). Rather, this great Archangel is responsible for leading us through our current ascension process to the paradise that is our divine inheritance.

The Angels vibrate through a unique consciousness, available for our sacred requests, and living the vectors of the universal law of attraction. They wait to act on the requests arising from deep within our hearts and souls. Their intention is to bring forth the information that 'now' is the time for the Angels to help shape the fortunes of all. Therefore, allow Metatron to be the great companion Teacher of your life. For Metatron's energy will heal any challenge, transmute any holding point, release any fatigue. Deduce the issue and simply give it up to this great One.

Atla Priest-Scientist Amun

During the end times of Atlantis, AMUN colonized the area we currently know as Central Mexico as many of the teachers moved into a lower vibration forgetting their psychic powers. The Communion of Amun's teachers eventually became the Aztec peoples who held, deep within their traditions, an ancient belief that they once arrived from a mythological place known as Aztlan. In fact, the Nahuatl language spoken by the Mesoamerican people reveals that Aztec means 'the people from Aztlan' or Atlantis.

During the colonization of Mesoamerica, Amun became the great creator God Quetzalcoatl – 'the feathered serpent' – governing the tribes who later became the Aztec and the Mayan, the planetary matrix, the Sun, the Moon and all the elements, just as he had in Atlantis. The name Amun literally means 'many Feathered Serpent', evoking a distant memory of Amun arriving from the skies, emblazoned in his own Merkabah's rays of light, like an erect plume of feathers.

During the Egyptian civilization, Amun was seen as the mysterious reincarnation of the Sun God Re or Ra, and is often depicted sitting on the throne of heaven, like a Pharoah covered by a crown of feathers or high plumes, just like Quetzalcoatl. In Egyptian, Amun means 'the hidden one', for this great Magician-teacher could morph into many forms to bring forth divine order on earth, through the people who were open to receive. Keeping in character, AMUN-RA, as the Lord of Concealment, had a mysterious presence, although the Egyptian people believed him to be a just and benign teacher. So much so that he was celebrated through metaphoric identification with all the Pharaohs – some of who took his name as theirs, as we see in the young Tut-Ankh-Amun.

In Greece, Amun took on the feminine role of the Gaia, who in Rome was known as Terra Mater. The Gaia was the broad-bosomed universal Earth Mother who had specific responsibilities as a primeval prophetess and keeper of the mysteries. Indeed, like Amun, the Gaia was considered the greatest of Oracles, and so she created the great centre at Delphi for the God Apollo to reside there. All the priests and priestesses who served at her Temples were the most renowned teachers and oracles, and were known as the sacred Sibyls, such as the wise Pythia and the devout Melissae who were great prophetesses of Delphi.

———————

Metatron's voice resonates deeply through this information and so, when Metatron as an instrument of the divine is called forth, should you be prepared for the mysterious forces that will be blown through your life. Change occurs when we are ripe for evolution, and if we attempt to hold back as a consequence of fear, or if we use our will to stop evolution, we also place limitations on the gift of creativity that is our true inheritance.

Instead we must trust life, trust Metatron, trust in Divine-will and, through faith, surrender to the flowing creativity of the wondrous universe. For in our illusory separateness, in our habit of isolation, in our fear of change, we forget that there is a bigger picture to the events that are unfolding, and this is a vision that is simply not unfolding or available for us to see in that given moment.

Metatron's wings of light overshadow you in these times, with a radiance more powerful than the spectre of your own darkness, and providing an augury that your force of creativity and your impact on the world are far more delightful than you ever believed, as much can be achieved both professionally and personally when patience, wisdom and prudence are evoked.

When Metatron's clarion harmonic rings through your life, this means that it no longer serves you to have unconfident reservations about yourself, it is no longer necessary to hold limited views about your abilities. Instead it is time to evolve even though the future seems intangible before you. Heaven knows what is in store for you, for only the Source knows best, but certainly it is time for you to recognize your unique potential in creation of the harmony and happiness that your soul so richly deserves.

The TEACHERS Communion values may be seen as:

1.   The ability to believe in the probability of the miraculous
2.   A tendency to seek out divine intelligence
3.   An ability to be merciful and compassionate
4.   An instinct for the energy of magic and intuition
5.   A yearning for the freedom of truth, growth and education

6. The will to discover new ideas, new ways and new information
7. A deep desire for wise counsel
8. The propensity for supporting the development of other people
9. A profound recognition of spiritual practice
10. A fascination for mystery and the rituals of spiritual faith
11. A profound ability to relinquish personal will into that of the Divine
12. An expanded vision of the sacred cosmology of life

AN ANGEL METATRON STORY

I was invited to stay in a sixteenth century Schloss in Bavaria, southern Germany, owned by a client of mine some years ago. The objective of my visit was to clear astral energy that appeared as unusual psychic phenomena, as observed by those living and working at the Schloss. The manifestations came in the form of spirits appearing in a certain part of the building, intense chilling atmospheres, and banging noises in the early hours of the morning. The belief was that these astral beings were the ghosts of a bygone era, that were caught between the worlds, and about which I was intrigued. Having served at a number of cord cutting processes, I was somewhat aware of what needed to be achieved.

On my arrival at the Schloss, the building looked spectacular, surrounded by thousands of hectares of pine forest, perched on a mountainous outcrop of granite, and with a beautiful waterfall captured in the landscaped alpine garden. The current building's granite stone structure was late seventeenth century, and possessed a number of superficial additions that had been tastefully added throughout the past hundred and fifty years. These had been achieved largely through the need to bring the internal living space forward in time to a modicum of twentieth century comfort.

In the light of the setting sun, the building's energy and external atmosphere deepened and yet, as I entered the building, the interior atmosphere felt undisturbed. Indeed, before the evening dinner, I was taken on a tour of the building. Impressive and grand without ostentation, I felt the general ambience cheerful – except that is, for an upper landing in the main part of the Castle. This elevation was built around a Great Hall which had a large ornate wooden staircase leading to several upper galleries. These in turn became wings of the Schloss, where several bedrooms were located.

I was told that two hundred years ago the upper gallery was

where a former resident of the building had been struck by a sword and fell to his death. The tragedy had so affected his young wife that she had 'lost her wits', and similarly leapt from the high stairs onto the flagstones below, losing her life. My plan was to hold a vigil in that particular part of the gallery during the night, so as to heal the spectral energies that appeared.

My host possessed an avid interest in supernatural phenomena, and had once employed a team of German psychic investigators to investigate the phenomena. The team had reported unusual electromagnetic energy in the gallery, and had taken several interesting photographs of light formations. They had also recorded feeling a sense of horror, but were not able to conduct any 'transitions of energy through cord-cutting' for their employer who had then spent much time attending to business interests in the USA.

After dinner, and when two other guests had retired to bed, my host and I sat in vigil until two o'clock in the morning, but no energy stirred. I was feeling tired after the travel of the day, and so suggested we retire for the night. My host agreed, and this we did. However, at four o'clock I was still awake, preoccupied by the location of these psychic activities. So taking a candle I moved along the dark corridor, calling both Archangel Michael & Metatron to me with as much force as I could muster. I simply knew intuitively that, on this night, I would need their love and companionship. My prayer to these great watchers of my life was:

A prayer to Michael and Metatron

Dear Archangels Michael and Metatron,
Please protect me in peace through this night of vigil.
Please carry me through the vale of shadows, and do not let the darkness arrest me.
Please aid my whole being as I bring light to this place, make courageous my mind, strengthen my heart with your love, and make robust my soul with your divine love.
With your ecstasy, please guide these dear ones to their rest, and draw their spiritual guardians forth to accompany them into light, for they are sorely in need of rest.
Let no darkness pass this way, and let the plan of love and light work out, whilst you seal the door where all evil dwells.
Let Light and Love restore the plan on Earth.

So be it.
Amen

Speaking this prayer, I moved along the corridor to the gallery, and immediately knew something else was energetically occurring that hadn't been apparent earlier. The atmosphere was very chilled, a smell of sulphur filled my nostrils, and I saw several light emanations of elemental beings around the supposed scene of the tragic happening. After about thirty minutes, I had a powerful sense of something I can only describe as dread and grief accumulating in my body, and I held the candle, prayers and bell I use closer to my heart.

These are reminders of our divinity, these tools of bell, book and candle, and I always take them with me and, on this occasion, I drew them more closely to my heart, and said this prayer:

A PRAYER TO ANGEL METATRON

Dear Archangel Metatron,
Please spread your bright light with such intensity through this space.
Please bring me your gift of divine intelligence, and allow my force of love and light to conduct safe passage to these dear beings, so that they may find their way back to the light.
Through your divine will, please draw them into the light of succour and healing, and allow me to chant safe passage for them, so that the dear spirit guardians who await them take them into the love that is the Source.
Please teach me to transform these beings into gestures of love and peace, and bring your all-seeing presence and wisdom to my aid.
I surrender myself to each moment of breath as a reflection of the divine.
With love, so be it.
Amen

I said this prayer three times, and noticed an extraordinary change of energy taking place in front of me, as the beautiful diamond Orb of Metatron came forth and filled the space around me with a love so sublime that tears moved down my face. After several minutes of this, the entire energy of the space became very still and I heard several high harmonics and crackling static, whilst an immensely chilling force moved through my body, and I felt the pain of 'their' sadness whilst this force passed through me to my eighth Chakra and beyond into the unquenchable light. The spirits of these two passed, and I chanted OM seven times, burning frankincense to sanctify the space. Later, the area of the house smelt beautiful and felt peaceful as though etheric rose oil were filling the whole gallery and staircase.

I hasten to add I don't usually conduct such ceremonies alone, and yet felt on this occasion that all my energies were guided by my Angelic companions. Please do not attend to similar circumstances unless you really know what you are engaged in.

To conclude, having stayed in contact with my German client, I hear that, subsequently, there have been no sounds or sights of unusual psychic activity in his Schloss.

A daily affirmation to draw Metatron's force

May I be made wise
May I be merciful
May I be intuitive
May I live in peace

A meditation for becoming at one with Metatron's Presence

1. Find yourself in a sacred space, whether this be a natural landscape, or your meditation room
2. Light a candle, burn some Frankincense (Metatron's scent), and play ambient music to consecrate the space with pure intention
3. Having consecrated the space, breathe in and out your intention to be in the presence of Metatron throughout the space and, if you possess a Diamond or Quartz Crystal, hold it in your hand or, if lying down, place it on your heart Chakra
4. Align your spine, and create a Mudra by placing your thumb and forefinger together. Feel your whole presence vigilant whether you are sitting or lying down
5. Breathe deeply with the breath-light moving through your whole being. Feel SILENCE, SOLITUDE and STILLNESS, for the latter will nourish your soul
6. Breathe deeply and sound OM through your heart chakra seven times; this will draw Metatron's presence into your energy field
7. Rest and notice how pure force extends from your heart into the

space before you, by seven feet (2m). As your force intensifies, imagine a beautiful DIAMOND Orb or ray of light emerging from the ending of your heart's vector. This is the force of the Angel Metatron. Then rest and listen to the Oracular whisperings of this Angel's magical presence, full of divine intelligence, miracles and mercy. As you meditate, you will feel the supernal light of the seventh dimensional energies of the Archangelic kingdoms loving and healing you

Namaste

MICHAEL

COSMIC LEADER

"The heart's song is the echo of your soul's note."

FIVE

AΠGEL MICHAEL

Illuminated by the Violet Ray of the Source, Michael is seen in the icon above, embraced within the form of the Egyptian God Thoth, in consequence of their closely aligned relationship, for they both embody the art of Alchemy.

Michael is essentially positioned in our lives as the leader of the Angels of Atlantis, transmuting all ills and lasering into our dominions, our lives, and the very substance of our flesh. Michael comes to lead us in the expiation and atonement of all karma, all sense of self-doubt, and all feelings of self-inflicted emotional pollution. Like Thoth, Michael uses the integrity of the heart as a dialing force, to lovingly assist integrity to take full lodging in one's life.

As the Ibis-headed Thoth, we see Michael depicted in the 'weighing of the heart ceremony', a solemn rite practiced as the soul passes into the afterlife through the Halls of Truth. These Halls were overseen by Matt, the Goddess of Truth, and accompanied by her husband, the God Thoth of the secret violet wisdom.

In the ancient legends, the sacred Egyptian Ibis was believed to have created life on Planet Earth by the laying of a beautiful egg and, as Thoth was considered an archetypal creative presence, the Ibis hitherto became associated with him, and was propagated thus by the High Priests of Hermapolis, the Temple of Thoth in Egypt.

Symbolically, the sacred Ibis wears black and white feathers, representing the notion of the eternal balance between light and dark, good and evil, right and wrong. This is the divine force that crystallizes Thoth's teaching on the dualistic energies of Planet Earth, for our planet is a binary planet, where nothing exists in singularity, all is plural. And so Thoth taught that ultimate freedom exists in the still-point of enquiry, resting between the two poles, the epicenter of the antithese. Therefore the Ibis, as a bird of creation, symbolizes the central axis of truth with its beak spearing any illusion, untruth, or mis-creation.

Similarly, Angel Michael is depicted slaying a dragon by piercing his spear into the body of the beast – a role that was later appointed to St. George. For the dragon of western culture pervades through the mists of time as the spectre of evil, with the face and body of the demonic. Similarly, the dragon masquerades as the serpent in the Garden of Eden, presenting Eve with the fruit of the tree of knowledge, and inveigling her loss of innocence.

Furthermore, the dragon represents the notion of both our individual and collective shadow. It symbolizes all that is perfidious in the nature of humanity, in all that wills us to be confounded and confused so that we give away our true power to the egoic tendencies of life. Michael brings ultimate wisdom to the vanquishing of the ego. Michael brings the notion of divine creative power to the fore. Michael cuts through any illusion, creating balance, patience, and the development of our personal sovereignty known as the great I AM PRESENCE.

Michael works closely with Metatron,and they are often depicted sharing similar responsibilities: stopping the hand of Abraham who was about to slay his only son in sacrifice to God; appearing to Moses in the burning bush; and rescuing Lot at the destruction of Sodom. Indeed, the legends associated with Archangel Michael as a transmutation healer in the Islamic, Jewish and Christian religious doctrines are so numerous that this refined Angelic force has been a major contributor to millions of lives, irrespective of cultural heritage.

Michael as a Cosmic Prince is the truly splendid ubiquitous leader offering wisdom, love, transformation and truth, and is ultimately often aligned with the energy of the Christos, the anointed Son of God.

Communion of the Leaders

In Atlantis, Michael served the communion of the LEADERS – the beings that gave the role of leadership to the promise of the cosmic experiment known as Planet Earth. They were the men and women who gave expression to a unique formula, a grand design that had been initially communicated through the inter-galactic council and orchestrated through the planetary matrix to create the golden civilization of Atlantis.

These LEADERS led the people of Atlantis to uphold the virtues of the eternal jewels that had been given and which brought a super-coherence between human and divine. These jewels arose from the bubbling brook of pure feeling – fresh, pure, clean and true – and, when quickened by the velocity of their own creativity, became waterfalls of love, compassion, empathy, wisdom, patience, non-judgment, forgiveness, gratitude and truth: Michael was the champion of these mercies.

Atla Priest-Scientist Osiris

The great Atla Priest-Scientist of the communion of the leaders was OSIRIS, the mighty leader of universal power, creativity, and the fertile force of life. Osiris brought the force of the CROWN CHAKRA to special dedication in the Temple worship, for the energy centre of the crown was seen as a chamber of renewal in the continuing cycle of life, and in the resonating conviction of the soul. The most salient objective that sprang from this created integration, liberation and freedom from suffering as the primary aims of Atlantean life.

The Violet Ray of this chakra portal represented the zenith of the seven personal Chakras and, through this energy centre, 'light' was transported into the trans-personal upper Chakras, the eighth through to the twelfth. Thereby a link was established between the nature of our three-dimensional bodies and the higher celestial realms, for this Chakra allows light from the Source to literally pour into the physical geometry of our being, bringing a connection to the super-conscious mind, the higher self, cosmic consciousness and, ultimately, God.

In ancient Egypt, Osiris was proclaimed as a Universal God who provided magnanimous leadership with his sister Isis as Queen, alongside Thoth as Scribe Messenger. Osiris led a golden age of prosperity in pre-dynastic Egypt, having drawn the elements and forces of nature into his governance. Then, having completed his governance, Osiris's son Horus led the nation forward, as Osiris moved his influence to reign as Sovereign Leader of the Underworld.

The Egyptians believed that Osiris ruling the underworld symbolized the continuation of life after death, for his new position assured that the underworld would be illuminated by solar light. Osiris radiated stability, confidence and power, illustrating the possibility of how a self-assured individual can transcend and survive life's challenges.

In order to embody Michael's values or characteristics, please ask yourself:

1. Am I open to the greatness of my potential power?
2. Am I sustained by the notion of life's enchantments?
3. Does my love flow as an aspiration of self-worth?
4. Am I honouring the power of my life's choices?

5. Am I fearful or joyous about being the master/mistress of my destiny?
6. Is my sense of self-empowerment open to receiving Michael's messages?
7. Do I want my life to be rich with new creative opportunities?
8. Can I be a Leader of the core elements of my life?
9. Do I live the probability of my life pulsing with light?
10. Am I fearful of asserting myself in social situations?
11. Is my life open to the creative flow of the Universe within?
12. Do I hide my powerful potential from the world?

Ponder these questions. Celebrate Michael as the God force within you, and hear the chords of sacred information directly communicated to you. Trust your psyche and, using your heart as a dowsing instrument, you will receive direct transmission from this cosmic Leader. These teachings will fill your life and soul with such awe and joy that you will desire to further your connection with Michael's force, just as was lived in Atlantis.

In the current era which draws us through the gateway of the Aquarian Age, the substance and essence of leadership is being fully investigated, largely because the models associated with Leadership, the ruling eminence of our past establishments, is no longer effective. For many of us are too negatively exercised by a love of power, injustice, aloofness and exclusivity.

Instead, we must turn to the creation of a new paradigm where leadership is based on the precepts of a more visionary, enlightened and emotionally intelligent force. In this, the enlightened leaders of the future are fully escorted by Michael, and radiate, generate and cultivate personal confidence and charity wherever they move, which in turn means they move everyone else. Their presence inspires other people to choose the highest choice, and thence other people's passions are fired to the limit of their force. The enlightened leaders enable this because they live a fully embodied state, exploring logic and intuition as two sides of the same process. Living thus means their presence illuminates the present.

When we attempt to define their power, we may record their strategic abilities, their management power, their vision, their people skills and their intelligent use of contemporary notions. However, truly enlightened leaders live a more primal note – they encourage us to feel our own emotions through the empathy of their own force of being.

When leaders of this calibre mobilize their people or create fundamental strategies, they mostly operate through purity of action and clarity of thought. They possess the courage to sail against the current wave of thought, perceiving the optimum potential for their people, at home or within the workforce. Their illumination is not *what* they act upon, it is *how* they achieve success, for they initiate their primal note feelings in the most appropriate of ways, by being fully honest with direction.

The key to this is simple – enlightened leaders function through emotional intelligence – they are essentially intelligent about their emotions, inspiring others to stimulate their own self-awareness, through charitable contributions to public welfare. This scintillating quality occurs as a consequence of the fact that they observe their own beings and relationships with care and open-heartedness. In this, their impact is as a guiding star for all.

The chemist [the enlightened leader] who can extract from his heart the elements of humility, compassion, respect, mercy, patience, joy, truth, forgiveness and peace, then compound them into one, can create the atom called LOVE

– KAHLIL GIBRAN

The Greek God Zeus

During the end times of Atlantis, the archetype of the Atlantean Priest-Scientist of the LEADERS firstly took the form of the Egyptian OSIRIS, and then transformed into the great Greek God Zeus, or Jupiter the ruler God of Rome. In ordinary men and women, the Zeus archetype forms the person whose driving force is to establish a kingdom in which his or her authority and power is fully exercised.

Therefore, the person aligning with this archetype would rather be his or her own boss than work for someone else. The Zeus archetypal character desires to work alone or with other powerful people in mutual agreement, and excels at summit meetings, forging alliances that determine clear boundaries.

Michael overshadows this form of leadership, and inspires us to apply these idiosyncrasies to our lives, encouraging us to live out our true spiritual authority through the sovereignty of the I AM PRESENCE. This is when we find our own throne and kingdom, for we all have the power of the Creator within us. Secondly, we discover our soul's purpose, and allow ourselves to be initiated into the world as a spiritual seeker, even though we may be disregarded by others simply because the Divine can be missing from other people's lives.

Michael wishes you to sit on the throne of your own true power, and in the universal wisdom of the one mind with visionary zeal. This is the moment when divine compassion will move through you, and alert you to understand that what you see without is also within. If we can feel the throne as a majestic seat of empathy, we not only surf the wave of our current use of personal power from a compassionate perspective, we also draw the experience of the past into the expression of the future as matter for the expression of love.

The LEADERS communion values may be seen as:

1. The ability to believe in oneself as a motivating force
2. A tendency to rely on one's personal counsel, and that of God
3. The ability to be measured and soulful in search of the integrity of others
4. An instinct for the energy of intuition, initiation and abundance
5. A yearning for the freedom of success and evolution
6. The will to discover new ways of being and doing
7. A deep desire for companions of similar personal might and experience
8. The propensity to support the development of people, but from an eagle's eyrie position
9. A profound recognition of the Divine Will behind all temporal gifts
10. An interest in the need to be patient, understanding and sustainable
11. A profound ability to seek out stability and security
12. An expansive belief in longevity and transcendence

An Angel Michael Story

When first we met, Margaret had recently graduated from a London Business School with an MBA, and had already found an excellent job in a major bank. This was realized through the prestige of her Graduate School, her excellent personal profile, skills and interview techniques. Margaret had sang-froid and style. Therefore she had excellent management potential, for her strategic intelligence, courage, forthrightness and leadership qualities were self-evident; yet she found her life to be listless and empty.

The point was that Margaret felt her heart to be hollow, for

Margaret felt unstirred by the material substance of life, and deeply sought a magical pulse that appeared absent. Literally nothing temporal seemed to move her.

I asked Margaret to come to one of the Angelic Atlantean Retreats I hold in the Dominican Republic, and she agreed. The time we spend on retreat is an opportunity to truly embody spirit through the SEVEN STEPS TO HEAVEN: the sacred sacraments the Angels have given me. These rituals provide us with an opportunity to examine the areas of our lives where we are not whole, where integration needs to take place, and so any 'energy holdings' are fully identified. Then, by the nature of the law of transmutation, the holding is transformed – physically, emotionally, mentally and spiritually. The end result is a much higher vibration for the individual, when vitality, well-being, self-empowerment and pure sustainable joy flow through the person, translating the energy of the thousand natural shocks that flesh is heir to. I often suggest that the Retreat is located in paradise, with a destination that is pure heaven.

One day, during a wonderful exercise I call 'Heart Dowsing', which was given me by Angel Michael and in which we honour each other for the beings we are, the group divided into partnerships for the initial part of the exercise when one person is to observe the other sitting before them. This requires sensitivity and concentration, for there is no 'doing', just 'being' with the person before one.

To begin with, Margaret found this extremely challenging and just couldn't surrender, wanting to control the situation. She felt uncomfortable about the loving scrutiny received from her female partner. After twenty minutes of immersing in the energy, which requires us to really surrender, moments of very deep sharing are experienced. Then through tender conversation, observations are made about what happened. These are moments of true grace, when the individuals speak of how their partner transmogrified before them, taking on different human shapes and characteristics – as if one was seeing the many incarnations of that being.

I then ask each partner to take turns in placing their left hand on the heart centre of the person in front of them, who by now is feeling extremely tranquil and full of light. I ask the person who is dowsing to whisper what sounds are heard from the background and foreground of this interaction. Generally people start to identify the bird song, the wind in the palm trees, the insects, the sound of the ocean waves, and then become aware of the heart-beat of the observed: calm, easy, constant and free flow, but which requires an even deeper letting go.

I then ask the person who is observed to increase the beat of their heart by feeling the excitement of joy, and for the observer to perceive what occurs. Mostly, it is observed that, as soon as the heartbeat increases with excitement, the sounds in the background synchronize with the sounds in the foreground, especially of course with the heart-beat.

Whether this be the cicadas, the flow of pranayama in the oxygen of the palm trees, the movement of the sub-tropical breezes, or the sound of the waves, everything falls into synchrony with the heart-beat and, when this happens, the energy field of the heart can become five thousand times greater than that of the brain. After we are sensitized thus, I ask the observer to tune their heart-beat to that of the observed.

This creates an utterly profound connection, and Margaret was so deeply moved as she felt the energy of creation moving into synergy with her heart that she felt palpable joy, merging, lifting, and soothing the experience of being utterly in sync with the whole of nature, and the whole of creation.

In these moments the range of surrounding harmonies caress and communicate their own truth, as they are all the one expression of the divine force of creation in the great Soul: effervescent, intensely light-filled, utterly true, completely charged by stillness, totally authentic, intimately connected, immensely loving, unequivocally healthy, and ecstatically happy. Margaret was immensely moved.

We took a break for water and fruit nourishment, and people quietly shared. Then a strange thing happened, when our intimate work together was disturbed by the noisy arrival of the Estate Manager's car. We observed him as he drove close to where we were in the Retreat House. On leaving his car he slammed the door and froze – he had left the keys in the car, and the doors had automatically electrically locked. He was stupefied by what he had done as the only keys he had were in the car. Nothing but magic would open the car, as a spare set of keys were not on the Island at that time.

I felt this was a perfect opportunity to utilize the sacred magic, and so asked some of the people of the Retreat to circle around the car, and to tune their heartbeats together by holding hands. This we did, taking time to breathe and establish contact with one another. I then asked everybody to see the beautiful violet ray of Michael exuding from their hearts, in synchrony with one another, and tune into the car, with the distinct intention of opening the car doors.

When the attunement had reached its optimum I said this prayer for us all:

A PRAYER TO ANGEL MICHAEL

Dear Archangel Michael,

Please fill me from the crown to the toe with your celestial light, allowing me to see my soul's core, and shape the destiny of my incarnation.

Help me to take charge of my spiritual growth, and to be the commander of my own frequency as my life unfolds.

Please purify my attention to see the constant flame of divine light within me, so that my being is always honed by unconditional love, and that I am God's servant here on earth.

In this moment, allow me to use part of my force to spring the keys from this locked car, so that once more the freedom of mobility produced by this vehicle can be used to bring joy and ease of flow to those people who utilize its power.

So be it.

Amen

We then stepped forward and five people placed their hands on the four door handles, and the trunk. Altogether, we said, "Please open the car with the sacred love of our intention" and each door opened freely, guided by Michael's extraordinary leadership force to achieve our objective.

We all shouted for joy – our creative intention had released the locked car, our breathing and heart dowsing together had created a unique bond between our heart chakras, and our heartbeat synchrony had brought about magic.

Margaret and I subsequently processed the whole conviction of this experience, including her profound awakening, and in her heart that day was born a new form of enlightened leadership, under the influence of Angel Michael.

A DAILY AFFIRMATION TO DRAW IN MICHAEL'S FORCE

May I be patient
May I be enchanted
May I feel powerful
May I live in peace

A MEDITATION FOR BECOMING AT ONE WITH MICHAEL'S PRESENCE

1. Find yourself in a sacred space, whether this be a natural landscape, or your meditation room
2. Light a candle, burn some Rose (Michael's scent), and play ambient music to consecrate the space with pure, loving intention
3. Having consecrated the space, breathe your intention to be in the presence of Michael throughout the space and, if you possess an Amethyst piece, hold it in your hand or, if lying down, place it on your heart
4. Align your spine, and create a Mudra by placing your thumb and forefinger together. Feel your whole presence vigilant whether you are sitting or lying down
5. Breathe deeply with the breath-light moving through your whole being. Feel SILENCE, SOLITUDE AND STILLNESS for the latter will nourish your soul
6. Breathe deeply and sound *OM* through your heart chakra seven times; this will draw Michael's presence into your energy field
7. Rest and notice how pure force extends from your heart into the space before you, by seven feet (2m). As your force intensifies, imagine a beautiful AMETHYST Orb of light emerging from the end of your heart's ray. This is the force of the Angel Michael from Mercury. Then rest and listen to the Oracular whisperings of this Angel's magical presence full of leadership force, patience and magic. As you meditate, you will feel the supernal light of the seventh dimensional energies of the Archangelic kingdoms loving and healing you

Namaste

RAPHAEL

HOLY HEALER

"The act of healing is a loving move back to wholeness."

SIX

AПGEL RAPHAEL

Atlantis and Angel Raphael dwelt together in sublime coherence. Each served the Universal force of the one and only splendour and, together through the alchemy of healing, brought emerald rays of utter inclusivity directly from the Source. This essentially fostered the notion that all healing is a movement back to wholeness.

When we seek Raphael, we are not taken to an outer domain but to that supreme place within where ultimately all is well and where all negativity is transformed. That place is the secret chamber of the heart – eternal, sublime, and absolute in the conviction of its Love. For this is the seat of the soul and reflects the great heart of the Cosmos.

Atlantis, as a cosmic project, was designed to bring higher states of consciousness to a different level of vibration, and altogether to a different perspective of cosmic creation, and Raphael, then as now, aided the constant fluctuations of rays from the galaxy. These potent forces penetrated the density of Earth's fabric and atmosphere in order to bring about the destined meeting between the Earth and the Divine and the fulfillment of an ancient prophecy. For it was designed that a fusion would be brought to fruition through a series of divergent, yet inter-connected forces, the utmost being the nature of duality – that nothing is singular, everything is plural – and so, through the nature of the Earth's bio-diversity, the planet developed its own particular relationship with the creative force of the Cosmos.

When we beseech Raphael for healing, we are not only healed but also vitally attuned to the frequency of pure flow from the Universe. For Raphael eternally emits an emerald ray of inspiration in loving care of the natural world, of all human beings and sentient life, and of course for the planet itself. For we are of the Earth, our nature mirrors the Earth, and to the Earth we return once our incarnation is complete.

Thus, Raphael's existence encourages us in the creation of that rare communion between the planet and our earthy nature. Healing in this sense means that we cleanse ourselves through the cycles of evolution determined by our planet's position in the Galaxy. For this localized area of the Cosmos is also perpetually growing so that God's plan is wrought. In this we see this Emerald Angel as the healing ray of the great God and Goddess at the centre of the Source.

For time immemorial, emerald has been treasured for its mystical properties and steeped in arcane lore. In the Bible, there is a reference to the Throne of God being exclusively made of emerald and, in Egypt, the God Thoth influenced his priest-scribes to write the sacred text of the Kybalion upon emerald tablets.

Emerald brings unity between opposites, emerald brings peace from conflict and healing from strife, it uplifts man from wrongdoing, and attracts the healing nature of the one and only force. The green colour of the emerald is reflected in the fourth chakra of the heart, the Anahata, and so significantly communicates the sacred intention behind the communion of the HEALERS on Atlantis. For the vibration of emerald green equalizes, calms, relaxes, encourages harmony, and keeps both mental and physical energy dynamically balanced. Green is essentially the colour vibration attuned to the harmony of the natural world and the welfare of the Devic realms.

Communion of the Healers

In Atlantis, Raphael's wings of Orb light overshadowed the communion of the Healers. This outstanding collective was governed by the great Atla Priest BASTET (also known as SEKHMET in ancient Egypt) and whose Temple was made exclusively from the emerald gem, localizing harmony within its walls, and producing a luminescent aura that stretched for a vast distance throughout the communion. This harmony stabilized the science of holography, allowing light to be recorded when filtering from an object which was then reconstructed when the object was no longer present. Much of Atlantean technology was created by this science, using light, colour and crystal, for communications, travel, construction, and information storage.

During the end times of Atlantis, Bastet took the people of her communion to Central Africa, to the lush-ness of the tropical forests that existed at that time around the lower part of the River Nile. In these locations, the Priesthood spent much of their time in meditation and healing as the planet had experienced several shocking disturbances during the great resolution known as the 'end times of Atlantis' when the planetary grid became severely imbalanced.

Atla Priest-Scientist Bastet

The Lion-headed Goddess of Bastet/Sekhmet was widely known in Ancient Egypt. Indeed, cats in general were considered sacred animals and, in the late period of this ancient civilization, physicians used the symbol of the black cat as a motif representing their healing arts. Bastet's energy was associated with fertility, childbirth, benevolence, intuition, marriage and, of course, healing.

Conversely, other stories exist depicting Bastet as a warrior lioness, aggressive, revengeful and savage, and it is written that her breath was of fire, which created the sands of the desert.

Ultimately, Atlantean lore saw the nature of the High Priest Bastet/ Sekhmet as a leveling force that brought about balance and harmony and, if you gaze at the great healing of the Raphael's icon at the beginning of the chapter, maybe you will ask yourself what Healer energy you possess.

The following questions may provoke the nature of RAPHAEL'S energy to move through you:

1. Are you open to the greatness of holistic healing?
2. Are you able to feel peace and tranquility moving through you?
3. Does your love always guide your nature?
4. Are you honouring the balances and boundaries of your life?
5. Are you open to being in deep communion with nature?
6. Do you cleanse your body, mind and soul regularly?
7. Do you want your being to be full of empathy for the life you sense around you?
8. Can you use your intuition to balance the dualities of life?
9. Is your life washed clean with the beauty of your love and that of the Universe?
10. Does your intention want to be woven into the cycles of nature?
11. Is your life open to the beauty and richness of the Divine Mother?
12. Do you regularly open yourself to the gift of love?

Temples of Healing

In ancient Greece and Rome, balance and harmony of body and spirit were of paramount importance, and the role of the great Bastet became venerated in the form of ATHENA in Greece and MINERVA in Rome. Athena, presided over battle in wartime and over the healing and domestic arts during periods of peace, and so functioned from an archetypal perspective as an inspiration for balancing the head with the heart in all situations, particularly those of an emotional nature.

In Atlantis, the central Temple for each communion was absolutely crucial, focusing the nature of the whole community's energy. However, there were also other temples of healing, created from nature weaving its own magic and enchantment in forest, rock, water and land formations. In these sacred places, the intention to venerate and celebrate was brought forth by creating a unity between the natural chemistry of the elements within the human body and the sacred vibration of the Divine.

These natural Temples were prolific, and were dedicated to a daily immersion in the energies required to stabilize immunity and create joyous well-being. They were founded on converging ley-lines, where watercourses wove their energies together, and where the Earth's energy matrix created interstices of potent connection. These were all suffused by love, and so created optimum healing for the Atlantean people who received the healing energies through their bodies as though they were conduits of excellence, from both the centre of the Earth and the outer limits of the cosmos.

Each of the sacred Temples based within the centre of the twelve communions was constructed in a circular shape, reflecting the divine feminine principle of inclusivity, and using ancient principles of geomancy. This art explores the realm where human consciousness meets in dialogue the spirit of the Earth, as well as empowering the harmonious interaction between a person and the place which enhances spiritual growth on all levels.

The interior of each temple was encrusted with precious or semi-precious gems, particularly those aligned with the rays of the dedicated Archangel, in this case the Emerald Rays of Raphael. At the centre of each Temple was placed the Crystal Skull of each communion, with a capstone Quartz crystal that anchored the inter-galactic force.

These powerful crystals assisted the people who lived within each communion, through the production of energy that brought the oscillations between sacred and profane, and between heavenly and earthly, into a consistency of harmonious intention. These 'capstone' crystals were extremely large, enabling them to hold the cosmic juice that stimulated the consciousness of each Temple.

The management of these amazing crystals – the orientation of what crystals were used in each building – was organized by special Crystal Keeper Priests; they were positioned to reflect the four natural elements:

NORTH – AIR
WEST – WATER
EAST – FIRE
SOUTH – EARTH

Each element aligned with the symphony of the gems that lived within each Temple. They amplified the sound, light and color waves, quickening the people who worshipped, and stirring the lives of those dear ones who lived abroad within the communion. Imagine the sound of fountains playing, wind chimes, crystals humming with certain harmonics, and large bowls of incense burning with exotic aromas, to have a glimpse of what each Temple's refined ambience would have been like.

Crystals are solidified sound, and were formed by a fusion of elements at high temperature millennia ago. When cooled, the crystals fostered vibrations that were transmitted from the intelligence of the inter-galactic counsel to Atlantis. For, you see, crystals have consciousness and enable intention to be made manifest in 3D by amplifying core thought.

Sound, colour, crystals and water were considered to be some of the principal components of spiritual nourishment for the Atlantean people. Each possessed a refined purity directly congruent with human form, enabling the higher vibrations of cosmic spirituality to more easily drench the flesh of the worshippers. In turn, the communions force was also enhanced by the Moon and the Sun, with season rituals that were observed and honoured.

As Atlantis evolved, the needs of the people also grew, and Raphael inspired and aided the evolution of these changes, particularly helping to develop sacred Sound Healing Temples. The proportions of these wonderful buildings fostered the acoustics which reflected the sacred geometry of each building. If the height of the building was in proportion to its length, a specific acoustic resonance was produced in alignment with this architectural geometry. We can see this today in many of our European medieval Cathedrals which were based on similar principles of sacred geometry, handed down through the Masons from time immemorial, and firstly utilized in Atlantis.

In each of the unique healing temples of Atlantis, there was constructed a portal at the top of the building. This vent allowed cosmic rays to enter, influencing the healing activities that took place such as psychic surgery, regeneration of cellular energy, and healing internal balances to generally tone the physical body. These rays were also amplified by the wonderful vibrations produced by the crystals, tuning the etheric body which regulated the Chakras, bringing peace, harmony and balance to the more dense physical body.

The Atlantean wisdom of preventative medicine, often contributed to by the use of herbal and aroma remedies, was similar to our contemporary healing arts of Ayurveda, Naturopathy and Homeopathy, but the Atlanteans used these efficacious processes to elevate their biochemistry while we tend to use them to eliminate toxicity.

The HEALERS communion values may be seen as:

1. A belief in the healing power of nature and the human body
2. The desire to create peace and harmony within, and therefore without
3. An ability to be measured and soulful in search of the integrity within all sentient life
4. A desire to find purity of purpose and clarity of direction in all natural things
5. A yearning for the freedom of evolution as a natural process within the Universe
6. A deep recognition of the complete inclusivity within the nature of holism
7. A deep desire to be guided by one's inner nature and higher self
8. The propensity for the empathetic healing of others
9. A profound recognition of the communion existing in all Divine creations
10. A broad interest in the art of cleansing, purification and transcendence
11. A profound interest in a search for beauty as an emanation of the Divine
12. An expanded comprehension about the healing that can be gained from the Earth's force and the power of the Cosmos

An Angel Raphael Story

Some time ago, the youngest member of a European Royal family was recommended to me for consultation. The request came for Angelic Sound Healing, and was made by a deeply caring member of the family whom I happened to know. They reported to me that the senior members of this family were very concerned about Letizia's challenges, as she had appeared disassociated from members of the family.

When I met Letizia, I discovered the enormity of her predicament as she confessed to me her long-standing relationship with cocaine. This she used to sustain levels of energy when feeling chronically depressed.

When we first spoke via the telephone, I encouraged Letizia to cease her cocaine habit by recommending a wonderful Psychotherapist I know at a major US Rehab Clinic. I had referred a number of young people to this therapist before, as I had discovered alcohol and drug addiction to be prevalent in a number of adolescents who had been drawn to my counsel. Letizia fully agreed to this intervention, and it was organized for her to access this wonderful clinic in the USA. I sent powerful prayers to Raphael that her healing be abundant and sustained.

Two months later when we met, Letizia looked radiant, sustained by a health regime that had been recommended by a fine nutritionist she had met at Rehab. The treatment had cleared her drug dependency, and Letizia's energy appeared magnetic, connecting with the deep Emerald Ray of Raphael the Healer. When I commented on this, Letizia told me about an experience she had, which dramatically persuaded her to follow through the suggestions I'd made.

After we had initially spoken, and whilst Letizia was still in Madrid, she had been chaotically moving around her apartment, looking for cigarettes to smoke, and cash to buy cocaine, when suddenly she had become aware of a green light emanating from her heart. Even though Letizia had not encountered preternatural phenomena before, she said that she was so moved by this energy, borne of such pure tranquility, that she stood in a full window of sunlight feeling the warm rays penetrating her body, which brought her health, sacred connection and an awareness of her own beauty – even though self-punishing behaviour had sabotaged this beauty for some time.

For several moments, she felt her 'abandonment issues' had completely evaporated, and that she was unconditionally loved by a tremendous supernal force she described as Angelic. This was the purest force she had ever encountered.

As she told this story, I saw her whole aura become surrounded by an emerald green light which touched her heart and drenched her body. This, I knew, was Raphael, and instantly gave great thanks for this loving administration from this great healing Angel of Atlantis. And, to this day, Letizia has been sustained by the blessed healing sent by Raphael, alongside the remarkable work of the Rehab Staff.

This is a prayer I recommended to crystallize Raphael's healing presence around Letizia, and therefore it may also function well for you if you require powerful healing from this powerful Angel.

A prayer to Angel Raphael

Dear Archangel Raphael,

I ask you for the Manna of your Divine Love which flows through you from the Infinite One.

May you bless me with your faith, cleanse me with your healing rays, and allow me to be a conduit for divine healing, so that I may lovingly serve the communion of the collective.

Please teach me ways of steadfast loving when faced with all negativity.

Please purge the fear percolating from my shadow, or from the collective shadow of my brothers and sisters, so that I simply transform all challenge and become a vessel of God's Love.

So be it,

Amen

A daily affirmation to draw in Raphael's force

May I be healthy
May I live a pure life
May I be cleansed from fear
May I live in peace

A meditation for becoming at one with Raphael's Presence

1. Find yourself in a sacred space, whether this be a natural land-scape, or your meditation room
2. Light a candle, burn some Lavender Oil (Raphael's scent or essence), and play ambient music to consecrate the space with pure, loving intention
3. Having consecrated the space, breathe your intention to be in the presence of Raphael throughout the space and, if you possess an Emerald or Malachite, hold it in your hand or, if lying down, place it on your heart
4. Align your spine, and create a Mudra by placing your thumb and forefinger together. Feel your whole presence vigilant whether you are sitting or lying down
5. Breathe deeply with the breath-light moving through your whole being. Feel SILENCE, SOLITUDE AND STILLNESS, for the latter will nourish your soul
6. Breathe deeply and sound *OM* through your heart chakra seven times; this will draw Raphael's presence into your energy field
7. Rest and notice how pure force extends from your heart into the space before you, by seven feet (2m). As your force intensifies, imagine a beautiful EMERALD ray of Orb light emerging from the ending of your heart's ray. This is the force of the Angel Raphael. Then rest and listen to the Oracular whisperings of this Angel's magical presence full of healing force, empathy and cleansing. As you meditate you will feel the supernal light of the seventh dimensional energies of the Archangelic kingdoms loving you and healing you through sacred communion with the Angels of Atlantis

Namaste

RAZIEL

DIVINE MYSTERIES

"To sense the mystery of the Angels
is to touch the soul of heaven."

SEVEN

AПGEL RAZİEL

Like the mysterious Pyramid and enigmatic Sphinx of Giza, Angel Raziel stands in vigil as the sacred Portal-Keeper of all time, positioned at the entrance to the Hall of Mysteries – the hall of divine wonder – because it contains the actual record of God's eternal truth and ultimate wisdom.

Ancient Kabalistic lore reveals Raziel as the Guardian Angel of Illumination, standing on Mount Horeb proclaiming the secrets of men to all mankind, and shining an iridescent ray filled with love and mercy. Indeed, Raziel's resplendent rays bring knowledge to all beings, guiding each soul's destiny through each incarnation and, for this, God has assigned Angel Raziel a very special role – as an agent of the secret regions and keeper of the supreme knowledge of the soul. Raziel holds a grimoire of divine wisdom in one ray of violet light and, in another ray, the crucible of eternal life shimmers.

Angel Raziel is known for giving Adam the Book of Knowledge after he and Eve had eaten of the Tree in Eden, which resulted in their expulsion from the garden. Another Hebrew tradition suggests that this action incited revulsion in Raziel's fellow Angels who took the book from Adam and threw it into an ocean. The Almighty One then restored the dripping book to Adam, through the agency of the God Neptune, whom we will meet later in this chapter. For this action, Yahweh drew Raziel into favour, and placed him on the left side of His presence.

Communion of the Mystery Keepers

With these special attributions, Angel Raziel oversaw the Atlantean communion of the MYSTERY KEEPERS, whose Temple was governed by one of the great High Priests, ANUBIS, whose responsibility was over the glory of death. Human life was seen as a small portion of cosmic existence, incarnated to live as thought made manifest, within a planetary domain constituted as a space-time continuum, and before returning to the eternal nature of consciousness – the ubiquitous reservoir of cosmic intelligence.

The temple of the Mystery-Keepers was a circular dome shaped building, with interior walls of white, encrusted in Obsidian, Moonstone and Quartz Crystals. These powerful crystal transformers were positioned to develop and enhance the intuitive and psychic gifts of the communion dwellers, and to elevate the amazing rituals that were held each day, and especially on each Full or New Moon – to help the evolution of the spiritual gifts possessed by the communion people. These rituals allowed all to envision infinity itself.

Nebhet, the Goddess of the Moon, was revered in Atlantis, not only as a light in the shadow darkness of life on Earth, but also because she governed the waters of the planet and aided the super-conductivity of feeling. Indeed, Nebhet often overshadowed the work of the Temple Priests and Priestesses who played a major part in the transitions that took place during the evolution of Atlantis, and towards the completion of this cosmic experiment. These holy ones possessed the formidable ability of oracular wisdom, seeing all things in the blink of an eye, so that each living being was naked before them.

Atla-Priest-Scientist Anubis and Noah

During the completion of Atlantis, prophecy after prophecy revealed the nature of the imminent cataclysm and the High Priest Anubis, with Angel Raziel, gave one of the Priests named Noah information designed to help him build an Ark. Noah was a great Avatar and knew how to summon the spirit of the elements, the spirit of the trees, and other beings of the elemental and nature kingdoms. These spirits were at one with him, and his soul's maturity granted him special powers to communicate with the natural world. Therefore, spirits performed certain functions at his behest.

The Bible story about Noah's 'exploits' verifies this. It records that Noah was one of the antediluvian patriarchs hundreds and hundreds of years old who, at the time of the great cataclysm, took much of the natural life of the great continent, particularly animal life, into a great ship which was destined to find the freedom of a new world.

This new world, promised to be free of the gross challenges that had been experienced in Atlantis during the times of 'completion' – an era that saw the misuse of political power, genetic engineering that corrupted the twelve helix DNA of human form, Priests abusing the power of the Great Tuaoi through the use of their psychic gifts, and collective negativity which created a tear in the subtle folds of the planetary matrix. This was so deleterious that there became a distortion of the twelve original Laws of the Universe.

When the violent earthquakes, tidal waves, and volcanic eruptions finally ceased, Noah dispatched his sacred cargo to an area we now know as Mesopotamia. Priests of Anubis then took the members of the Mystery-Keepers communion to both Mount Kailash in Tibet and northern regions of Egypt, two of the most powerful Earth energy centres where many of the ancient records of Atlantis are still kept in magic cache. These mysteries are now percolating into the consciousness of many human beings at this time of great change, the precessional Equinox.

When we bring Raziel into our lives through gentle praise and petition, when we are present to the magical sensitivity of this Angel, we also begin to feel the power of the mysteries seeping through us. They quicken our lives, creating extra-sensory sensitivity and a revivification of our psychic gifts. Thereby, telepathy, remote viewing, awareness of the elemental forms of life, observation of the air and land contours created by the ley lines of the planetary matrix and awareness of the melding nature of the space-time continuum – all begin to occur.

You may already have felt the probing ray of your consciousness observing magical processes such as synchronicity and psychic phenomenon. One of the most common is the sudden appearance of feathers on your path, for so many of our brothers and sisters see Angels as human beings with wings. In all simplicity, the spiritual terrain beyond that which you perceive as 'material' will broaden the vistas of your consciousness, and the depth of outer space will surpass your perspective, for it will be perceived as real, and from a position of no doubt.

This enhanced 'seeing' will provide you with a sense of your divine gifts pulsing in each moment of life, arousing that deeper part of your soul, which unfolds the very nature of your spirit, and the field of creation you see without – the great realm of infinity. This is a place of great adventure where Raziel connects us with a conduit of eternity that brings our souls to a sublime reckoning, the balm of healing that we know as inclusive love. This presence never diminishes,simply we have become distracted by years and years of dense busy-ness, where the paradigms of intellectualization and commercialization supersede the preternatural.

Raziel brings us to the core of our souls, and the visionary poet William Blake reminds us of this:

> *To see a World in a Grain of Sand*
> *And a Heaven in a Wild Flower,*
> *Hold Infinity in the palm of your hand*
> *And Eternity in an hour.*

When I was a child, Raziel was a constant presence in my life, particularly during my introduction to Christianity at St. James Church, Piccadilly, London. This church harbours a rare spiritual force, brought together by a fusion of sacred geometry, geomantic architecture, converging leys, and a sacred watercourse.

This was Christopher Wren's most loved temple of sound, built in 1684 after the great fire of London in 1666, when Wren was commissioned to rebuild much of the city. Wren commented on this Church as being "my favourite acoustic chamber after St. Paul's".

Many famous people were christened in the marble font at St. James's, including the poet and visionary William Blake and, as a small child, I saw his presence there, so that when I'd reached an age that permitted understanding, I avidly read his works, and lovingly perused his beautiful illustrations and paintings. The significance of Blake's informative creativity and Raziel's mysteries unite in much of his creative outpouring, where his profound teachings of life abound in observations of the preternatural world. Blake lived during the era we now know as the Romantic Period, when industrialization was beginning to sully the beauty of the natural world, which had always been seen as a reflection of God's breath and spirit. The following lines of Blake reflect this:

> *We are led to believe a Lie*
> *When we see not Thro' the Eye*
> *Which was born in a Night to Perish in a Night*
> *When the Soul Slept in Beams of Light.*

Whereas, if we can only hold firm to the conviction that:

> *He who Doubts from what he sees*
> *Will ne'er believe, do what you Please.*
> *If the Sun & Moon should doubt*
> *They'd immediately go out.*

I believe we are now returning to be in awe with the nature of Raziel's presence. This wonderful Angel quells all doubt, for Raziel is enraptured by the very font of God's creation, and asks us to pledge that all experience be derived from belief in the sacred mysteries. This ensures God consciousness within us, for Raziel oversees the secret chamber of our heart knowing that, when we choose to enter the magic of life, the veils of illusion are parted, and what is revealed defies the rational mind, for we see life truly as a force of infinity. Then the experience of life fuses with the knowledge of the afterlife, as intuition becomes conscience. Thus so, Raziel leads us to the Halls of Truth governed by Maat the Goddess of Truth, and Anubis the God of the Afterlife.

Ask yourself the following questions, and the answers will alert you to whether the nature of Raziel's energy moves fully through your life. When you petition Raziel, the force of this resplendent Angel will automatically help you transform your life:

1. Am I open to believing in the magic and mystery of creation?
2. Am I able to sense the depth of my in-tuition?
3. Does my soul or higher self guide my daily living?
4. Am I honouring the cycles of nature that determine the life of the planet and the Cosmos?
5. Am I conscious of the fruits of my own magical awareness?
6. How often do I meditate and consider the power of retreat?
7. When do I bring an awareness of infinity into my day?
8. Can I use my intuition to penetrate deeper into understanding human nature and life's mysteries?
9. Is my life oriented by faith in goodness, truth and wisdom?
10. Does my consciousness wish to serve my brothers and sisters?
11. Is my mind open to the possibility of completely re-arranging my reality?
12. Do I attend daily to a balance between my rational and intuitive mind?

Einstein said:
The intuitive mind is a sacred gift, the rational mind a faithful servant. We have created a society that honours the servant and has forgotten the gift.

And yet, if we can open ourselves to the paramount conviction that Raziel is present in our lives to help us with the balance of the inner and outer – just as the High Priest Anubis taught the unification between the conscious and unconscious aspects of human life – we move into a greater understanding of our love, of our spiritual intelligence, and of the path our soul wishes us to take to optimize our creative energy towards the creation of a paradise full of extraordinary opportunities.

Anubis and Healing

In ancient Egypt, Anubis as the Lord of the Afterlife was considered to have special healing gifts. For example, when a human spirit passed, they were summoned into the Halls of Truth and Judgment so that the heart of the deceased could be weighed against the weight of a feather, before Osiris and Maat. If the heart proved to be heavier than the weight of the feather, a creature named Ammut would appear, and devour the heart. If the heart was lighter, proving the integrity of a life lived full of love, Anubis would offer companionship to the spirit in transition, who would then be taken by Osiris into paradise.

Indeed, for any of us who has been through 'the long dark night of the soul', we remember the person who was present to our predicament, the one that was rather like Anubis; the dear one who held the space, as we crashed deeper into the depths of our emotional chaos, wherever or whenever the darkness became most intense. And, just as it is darkest before the dawn, we felt provided for by their insights, even if the fullness of their teachings didn't 'dawn' on us until much later in life.

Raziel and Anubis augur healing, for they always provide safe passage, especially as we experience the death of an aspect of life that has outgrown us. This truly occurs if we see it is time to release self-limiting behaviour. This truly functions when it is time to see oneself as an expansive, self-empowered person. This truly opens when we acknowledge who we are at a quantum level of soul. For here we perceive an infinite ability to heal and transform our lives. Therefore being drenched in Raziel's and Anubis's energy means we open ourselves to the deep seams of our underwater, underworld, under-the-surface feelings, where feeling lives as the language of the soul.

The Greek God Poseidon

In ancient Greece, the domain of the ocean reflected the unconsciousness of man and the mysteries of the emotional body. These forces were held deep within the sea of energy comprised of Mother Earth's tears, and the God Poseidon, as a manifestation of Anubis, governed the emotionality of these ocean depths.

The oceans of our planet reflect the flood of our feelings and the deluge of our dreams that, within their watery vastness, give vent to the emotions and memories of life. Deeper still are the darker depths holding primeval creatures and myriad forms known as the collective unconscious, and overseen by the God Poseidon in Greece, or the God Neptune in Rome. These powerful beings were often fabled as reacting through intense emotions and primeval monsters who, whenever they were provoked, gave expression through earth shattering quakes and other natural disasters that displaced the activities of man, thus encouraging new growth.

Poseidon was also an archetype from which a psychological realm of great depth and beauty could also pour forth, from which creativity sprang. As William Blake wrote:

> *In what distant deeps or skies*
> *Burnt the fire of thine eyes?*

Poseidon's realm excites the person who is directly in touch with their emotions and feelings, for one who expresses feelings immediately, directly and spontaneously exalts in the pulse and breath of life. Conversely, deep feelings can also be harboured by the introverted, waiting for expression until healing is sought, through the floodgates opening. In either case, Poseidon provokes deep and intense interactions with life, encouraging questions to be asked that open the mysteries of passion, intuition, love and faith – and in a world that is emotionally repressed by the excesses of the patriarchal establishment, human emotion is rarely allowed to utter its truth, until we claim its powerful right to live.

The MYSTERY KEEPERS communion values may be seen as:

1. A belief in the wisdom of dreams and intuition
2. A desire for retreat to examine and reflect on the soul
3. The ability to seek belief, faith and trust as the expressions of soulful love
4. A conviction in the soul's eternal evolution through life
5. A yearning to communicate the essence of one's spirituality
6. A deep recognition for the sanctity of life in all animate forms
7. A respect for the rituals that allow us to experience the sanctuary of the soul, through grace and truth
8. A profound belief in the mystery of love, and the desire to pulse with its verve

9. A loving respect for the ministry and agency of the Angelic communion
10. The wish to discover the secrets of God in human nature
11. A way of living the principles of faith in Divine Will
12. A search for that which upholds a search for the utmost good in all things

An Angel Raziel Story

Many years ago, a particularly impressive female client requested a Past Life Regression. This client was an eminent PR specialist from South America and, although she possessed a very prosperous business both in New York City and in London, she was also acutely aware of the spirit of life, and alert to the possibility of reincarnation. So she avidly sought information about all aspects of her soul's journey.

Valeria had a recurring dream of some magnitude and yet, each time she experienced this deep, lucid dream, the finalization of its journey was always vague and uncertain and included a feeling of being torn from something prized and of great value. The scenario in the dream was dramatic, and associated with a kingdom of activities that she felt were either from the future, or of a past civilization that had advanced technology, but was unlike anything that the history books purport to exist.

In her dreams, Valeria experienced an acute sensation of floating in an aircraft, and since she knew the ancient Greeks didn't have ships which travelled effortlessly through the air, she was intrigued by the fact that the clothes she wore in the dream were similar to those depicted on the Greek Amphorae of antiquity.

The dream seemed to always occur around the cycle of the full moon, and Valeria was eager to regress in order to by-pass her conscious mind which, she felt, interfered with her intuition as a consequence of her busy work responsibilities; she genuinely wished to excavate the ancient memories held deep within her unconscious.

We began by exploring deep relaxation, using pranayama and internal viewing processes, to release tensions from each part of her body. Valeria very soon elicited alpha states that took her into deep theta consciousness – that area of our consciousness where we access hypnosis. Similarly, it was paramount to encourage specific intention in order to stimulate her unconscious – rather like using a map to travel through a terrain of memories, that helps to guide one through the landscape of millions of thoughts.

Valeria saw herself standing in a very large round, completely white, dome structure, except for the brilliant appearance of certain myriad jewels set into the walls and ceiling. She saw these as glistening lights, reflecting the brilliant moonbeams that poured as shafts of light through a central aperture in the roof of the building. The lights bore semblance of candles burning, except they revealed separate colours and, even though the one light of the moon shone through, each light appeared alive with a different force.

At the centre of this large space, which she somehow knew to be a Temple of Healing, was a three-metre high Obsidian crystal surrounded by other Quartz crystals, appearing as though they were different parts of a whole. She was also aware of exquisite tones emerging from each crystal, which created a wonderful symphony that filled the space – the very soul of the Temple. Incense of the violet flower burned, filling the air with an aroma that was so intoxicating that it aided her ability to see all before her, as a psychic reality.

Three Priests stood in the centre wearing long white cotton robes, similarly bejeweled with small obsidians, moonstones and diamonds, shaped in patterns which, she knew, intrinsically reflected different parts of the galaxy. There was a sense of being in the material energy of Planet Earth, as well as being in an intense relationship with the cosmology of the galaxy.

Peace pervaded the whole scene and those present felt serene. Emerging from the central crystal was a large holographic image of a crescent moon, accompanied by hieroglyphic writing, and moving cylindrical space vehicles. These pulsated with millions of tiny lights in symphonic patterns, and Valeria knew that these crafts bore visitors from other worlds, called to this unique time and space to be part of this hallowed ceremony, at the centre of which would occur a lunar eclipse.

Suddenly, she became aware of an exquisitely large orb of Indigo light, as large as the building itself, hovering above the assembled group, with the ability to move through walls. Approximately three hundred people were present, all folded into extraordinary stillness, and shining with a powerful concentration of force. The Orb, Valeria knew, was Angel Raziel, the companion of the Temple, where the Priests and Priestesses focused their lives on the magic of the healing arts.

As the concentration of the group intensified, several crystals began to move slowly through the air of the Temple, forming a circle at some considerable height. As this occurred, Valeria felt her own body levitating, moving towards the aperture in the ceiling of the Temple. This wasn't threatening or dangerous, she simply moved on the currents of intention that emerged from the assembled group, amplified by the crystals, and she felt her body bathed in the overseeing beauty of Raziel's force.

Then, as she moved through the roof aperture of the building, a feeling of immense awe gathered within her as she saw the Moon high above her. Similarly, she became aware of a silver cylinder moving through space towards her, about three metres in length, and a metre in girth. As it approached her floating body, a door opened in the area of the craft that moved closest to the Earth, and overtones emerged that telepathically conveyed to her the name of Nerfitiha, which she knew was hers.

Revealed thus, her task was to enter the craft to receive an initiation from the Goddess of the Moon. Furthermore, an interstellar energy would be transmitted to her concerning a medicinal plant that would eventually burgeon on Planet Earth, bringing vast healing to many women in childbirth – the plant was to be called Ixkibix – and she entered the craft to receive the data.

At this point, Valeria was stirred deeply and began speaking a language I didn't recognize that sounded ancient and Elvish – a language of the elements – of water, wind and rocks, full of elongated vowel music expressed from the heart, and many clicking consonants. There was a sense that this was the Atlantean tongue, and I intuited Valeria was being given powerful information.

Later, she told me that the density of Planet Earth brought challenges to women during childbirth, even though they engaged in water births and were accompanied by Dolphins who appeared as wonderful midwives. Valeria said she was told many women remembered former lives from other planets when their bodies were extremely different and childbirth didn't occur. They lived their lives for eternity, having been formed from elemental forces.

At which point Valeria stirred deeply again, and I could see she was moving out of her hypnotic state, so I slowly brought her back to beta consciousness, aware of her physical surroundings. This had been an amazing journey for her, and after some time of recovery, she was able to tell me the whole story as she had encountered the experience. It was apparent that the dream had reached its conclusion, because she had never witnessed the sense of being taken into the spacecraft before, and of receiving such data.

———————

Perhaps other intuitions or dreams will occur to you, once you meditate on Raziel's Icon above, for it is apparent that this powerful Angel is speaking to us, encouraging us to touch deeper into the intuition of our own being. Perhaps you will need to spend time in nature, feeling the pulse of divine love moving through you, and holding you in its warm embrace.

Use this prayer, or perhaps one of your own creation to elicit Raziel's overt intuitive support. As you pray or chant, you will feel this wondrous Angel's warm embrace pouring through you; or you may suddenly experience an innate knowing of your own soul's wisdom about an outcome.

A prayer to Angel Raziel

Dear Archangel Raziel,

Please show me the elixir of your divine insight, and purify my intuition with the wisdom of 'creation' filled with beauty.

Please shine a light on the mysteries of my life so that full awareness dawns concerning the aspect of my soul's infinity, urging my love to embrace the role as a servant of creation.

Allow me to know this truth in the deepest part of my soul and body, so that I may carry the light wherever I may be.

Teach me to not stumble on my path, and remain woven within the conviction of the planetary matrix, which is supreme love

So be it,

Amen

A daily affirmation to draw in Raziel's force

May I be intuitive
May I live a life full of spirit
May I be made joyous by the awe of life's magic
May I live in peace

A MEDITATION FOR BECOMING AT ONE WITH RAZIEL'S FORCE

1. Find yourself in a sacred space, whether this be a natural land-scape, or your meditation room

2. Light a candle, burn some Violet Oil (Raziel's scent or essence), and play ambient music to consecrate the space with pure, loving intention

3. Having consecrated the space, breathe your intention to be in the presence of Raziel throughout the space and, if you possess an Obsidian or Moonstone hold it in your hand or, if lying down, place it on your heart

4. Align your spine, and create a Mudra by placing your thumb and forefinger together. Feel your whole presence vigilant whether you are sitting or lying down

5. Breathe deeply with the breath-light moving through your whole being. Feel SILENCE, SOLITUDE AND STILLNESS, for the latter will nourish your soul

6. Breathe deeply and sound *OM* through your heart chakra seven times; this will draw Raziel's presence into your energy field

7. Rest and notice how pure force extends from your heart into the space before you, by seven feet (2m). As your force intensifies, imagine a beautiful INDIGO Orb ray of light emerging from the ending of your heart's ray. This is the force of the Angel Raziel. Then rest and listen to the Oracular whisperings of this Angel's magical presence full of healing force, faith and intuition. As you meditate, you will feel the supernal light of the seventh dimensional energies of the Archangelic kingdoms loving you and healing you by the sacred Communion with the Angels of Atlantis

Namaste

SANDALPHON

SACRED GUARDIAN

"The mantle of the guardian is the rapture of the infinite."

EIGHT

ANGEL SANDALPHON

To feel the warmth of Sandalphon's loving amber Orb rays upon our expectant faces, let's first gaze on an incarnation associated with this Angel's shimmering force.

Many venerable Bible stories abound concerning the Prophet Elijah, who was considered 'great in the eyes of God'. For Elijah dedicated his life to the worship of Yahweh's Earth, and developed a spiritual passion that overrode the ninth century deification of the God Baal – an animistic deity considered mighty by the society of that time.

Elijah's unbending love, goodness, prayer and dedication to the one God of the Source was rewarded with the ability to raise the dead and bring forth fire from heaven. Indeed, at the end of his long life, Elijah ascended in a chariot drawn by horses of flame, which carried him into heaven, and so Elijah took the form of the Archangel Sandalphon, becoming even closer in communion with God.

There are parallels here with that of Enoch being graced by God's countenance, and ascending into heaven to become Archangel Metatron. In this respect, for thousand of years, the two Angels have been described as 'twin brothers', which accounts for the Greek derivation of the name Sandalphon – meaning 'co-brother'.

Both Archangels are linked in a partnership of celestial zeal for Sandalphon governs the transformation of the electrical energies that generate from the Earth, making connection with the Cosmic Matrix, whereas Metatron facilitates the magnetic energies drawn from the galaxy to Planet Earth, which create alignment with the Planetary Matrix. These dual forces flow through the form and symbol of infinity, circling within a figure eight, like a constant two-way flow of energy and information, looping as it were in rhythmic harmony between Heaven and Earth.

Spectacularly, they meet at the Earth's major centres of force – one such being Avebury Henge, Wiltshire, which exists as an open-air temple to the Divine Goddess Gaia – and which you will see in the Icon at the heading of this chapter. Sandalphon's especial relationship with Avebury brings to our lives, to the life of the planet and that of the cosmos, the remarkable healing energies of Cosmic Union.

Sandalphon is charged with vast spirals of Cosmic Light, condensed from the Source and destined to draw the energy of Planet Earth into the ascension force of the Galaxy. For this to happen, Sandalphon asks all Light workers to assist with this transformation. Both from a planetary perspective, in venerating the body of Mother Earth, and from the advantage of drawing energy into one's body, by feeling love, compassion, goodness, mercy and joy, these are essential tools to open the vectors of individual and planetary ascension.

> *Each time a person stands for an ideal, or acts to improve the lot of others, or strikes out against injustice, he or she sends forth a tiny ripple of hope. All of these ripples move into millions of different energy centers, and these daring ripples build a current that may sweep down the mightiest walls of oppression and resistance.*
>
> *– ROBERT KENNEDY*

In service to this great impulse, orchestrated by the monumental cosmic shifts that abound, leading us towards December 21st, 2012, we also see the Earth-elementals, the Devic-beings, and the In-dwellers of the Earth, joining us to raise planetary consciousness. All the secrets of the Earth are accessible through these sacred guardians of the planet and, through Sandalphon, will be dispensed when we are worthy to receive them, in respecting and understanding their power.

Therefore, we are asked to be vigilant and caring in our relationship with the Earth. We are requested to love the beauty of its bio-diversity, through eco-sustainable principles. We are asked to care for our physical bodies by eating water-based foods, and we are encouraged to love the environment so that our beings are sustained by its goodness, through and through.

Ask yourself these questions to draw Sandalphon's energy deep into the Earth of your being:

1. Am I responsible for the aspects of my life, which are of the Earth?
2. Am I able to feel the rhythms and pulse of Mother Nature?
3. Does my soul read the reason for my presence on this Planet?
4. Am I fully honouring the beauty of the Earth's environment?
5. Am I open to the Earth-Elementals and Guardians of Nature?
6. Do I regularly meditate in honour of this exquisite planet?
7. What can I do to increase the flow of love in direction to the planet?

8. Am I aware of the Fairy Kingdom that loves this planet?
9. What do I 'be' rather than 'do' for the evolution of Planet Earth?
10. What do I know about the planetary cycles of our Globe within the Galaxy?
11. Do I see my life as a brother or sister of the planet?
12. What legacy can I enrich the planet with, seeing the Earth as a planetary organism, and living the course of my life upon it?

Sandalphon is God's Guardian presence here on Earth, awakening the inner kingdom of creative purpose through which thought creates the energy of the world, where specific intention brings joy-filled achievement, and where purpose manifests untold riches. In this, Sandalphon considers the cycles of nature and the quantum waves of the cosmos as inter-related creative forces. Sandalphon inspires the essence of living in co-creation with nature, from the vantage point of the Brown/Amber Orb of Angelic proportion and, just like Elijah walking on Earth, refines and informs our search for the Divine in our human-ness.

Evolving currents of force through Sandalphon enable this great Angel to govern the Earth Star Chakra of we human beings, which helps give shape to our purpose on Earth from a Divine perspective, and therefore, as we open ourselves to Source energy, we restore the harmony of Planet Earth's consciousness. Then divine love becomes the Earth's loving force.

Through our planet's life, we see evidence of this chakra awakening in the current human interest in ecology, and the protection of Earth's sensitive surface and air. Like the Atlanteans before us, we are encouraged to live co-creatively with Earth Spirits and Mother Nature, so we become enlivened by the pulsations of Mother Earth through the Sun-Moon cycles – for we need to venerate these rhythms and pulses, as we would God and our own beloved ones.

Highly skilled Atla Priests governed the Atlantean Temple of the GUARD-IANS, existing in both Priest and Priestess form. Their unique meditations and rituals prepared their minds and bodies to hold the balance of force within the energy principles of Yin/Yang, Light/Dark, Sun/Moon, Cosmos/Earth.

Overseeing these operations was the High Priestess NUT, who covered the continent with her celestial amber presence, whilst her male form in the shape of the High Priest ATLAS held up the roof of the firmament with his earthy, brown sovereignty. Both Nut and Atlas were ancient spiritual celebrities, who lived rarefied existences whilst on planet Earth. Indeed, during the end times of Atlantis, they brought the richness of their Guardian Communion to the island of the Angles, the landmass know known as Great Britain.

Goddess Nut and God Atlas

The Goddess Nut in Ancient Egypt was the wife of Geb and the mother of Isis, Osiris, Seth and Nephthys – she was believed to have been formed from the firmament which protected the Earth and, as such, she maintained all that was and is in existence. Described often as the mistress of the heavenly bodies, her raiment was covered in gemstones from the different communions so that she refracted light from all heavenly and earthly dimensions, for she was the protective Mother to all mortal beings on Earth. Furthermore, Nut was thought to swallow the stars just before dawn, to give birth to the Sun at morn, and then at the end of day, she swallowed the Sun and literally gave birth to the stars for her heavenly pleasure. Atlas, the masculine presence of Nut, was considered to be a symbol of endurance, as he steadfastly held the Earth from collapsing into space.

In ancient Greece, Nut became the Goddess Hestia, and in Rome Vesta. Hestia was proclaimed the Goddess of the Hearth, symbolizing the archetype of the earthly function and of keeping the house in order, characteristics that emerge in people who acquire a sense of inner harmony whilst accomplishing daily tasks. And just like Nut's daily meditation of holding the heavens from falling on the Earth, Hestia centres and draws inner peace from the task in hand. She is like a person living within a religious order, for whom every activity is done 'in service to God.' So Nut and Hestia can be seen in human terms as the wise person and the inner mystic.

The Guardians of many sacred shrines and holy places are benignly overshadowed by Sandalphon's energy, which also rains beautiful amber rays on the growing number of eco-friendly projects that are emerging on the world stage. Two such projects are the well-established Findhorn Spiritual Community/Eco-village in Moray, Scotland and the newly evolving KI-RA in the Dominican Republic.

Working with Sandalphon means we develop greater respect for our planetary lives, and for the spiritual richness of the flora and fauna encompassing the Globe. For example, if you know anyone who has recently awoken from the trance-sleep of disconnection from their earthly nature, you can be certain that Sandalphon's kiss, like the fabled Prince of 'Sleeping Beauty', was implicitly involved in the process of their awakening. This 'kiss' cleanses one's connection with Earth, renewing the physical body through increasing draughts of solar and pranic energy, as well as aiding the development of a truly embodied and grounded spirituality. These are the individuals who become keenly aware of the environment, and develop a burgeoning sense of global responsibility.

The GUARDIANS communion on Atlantis espoused these values:

1. An allegiance to the power of Mother Earth and her cycles of nature
2. A constant respect for the health and vitality of one's body in reflection of the Earth
3. A love and honouring of Earth and the other planets as principles of eternity
4. A determination to be clear with intention as a symbol of being clear with life
5. An upholding of the notion of honesty and co-creativity
6. A deep recognition for the sanctity of life in all animate forms
7. A diligent regard for the cycles of the planet in regard to the Moon and Sun
8. A profound Guardianship for the peace and silence of the Earth Mother
9. A love of tenderness and strength, as they flow through human life
10. A desire to discover the secrets of spirit made flesh
11. A veneration of the eternal jewels of life such a grace and truth
12. An ability to constantly release the old in favour of the new moment of creativity

An Angel Sandalphon Story

A number of years ago, I was approached by the eighteen-year old daughter of a client, who had a very close relationship with Angel Sandalphon.

However, at our first meeting, Henrietta described her life as being meaningless. She had tested her boundaries whilst at school, through anti-social behaviour, limitless superficiality, gross over-partying, and constant confrontations with authority. Henrietta confessed that her life at school had been immersed in drugs and alcohol, in order to literally 'get out of her body'.

Henrietta looked extremely unwell – thin, depressed, unhappy, and with an aura that appeared as a pale shade of grey – in fact Henrietta confessed that her body felt completely listless. Yet, at the same time, Henrietta had experienced psychic episodes, including synchronicity, visions of spirit, extra-terrestrial energies, and déjà-vu. I listened carefully, and saw that she was finely connected with the elemental world – strangely her waif-like appearance gave strong impressions of the Devic world.

We talked at length about what she considered to be the dysfunctional nature of her family, within which she felt little love or succour, and I provided Henrietta with strategies to help her see ways of becoming physically robust and emotionally centred.

One of Henrietta's first options was to meet a sensitive Nutritionist I recommended for information about a clear health regime, and the second one was to begin a meditation practice, including daily Yoga or Pilates; she agreed, and loving support encouraged her to move more easily towards good health, vitality and balanced well-being.

After four weeks of restorative health regimes, Henrietta came back to see me and, looking so much better, she excitedly told me about the dreams she had whilst cleansing her body. One such dream was of walking an intense, sunny Spanish road for miles and miles (although English, she knew Spain well, and spoke the language), and felt sublimely happy about her journey, even though it initially appeared arduous.

Henrietta knew she must find out what this meant, as the way had been lit by a beautiful amber light that had left her feeling serene, and completely in connection with Mother Earth. So I revealed to her information about the amber light of Sandalphon's energy, suggesting that this force had been with her from the moment we had met – at which point she was extremely moved. Furthermore, we spoke of the pilgrimage of the Camino, finalizing at Santiago de Compostela in Galicia, North West Spain.

The Camino de Santiago de Compostela, also known as 'The Way of St. James', is a collection of old pilgrim routes covering the whole of Europe. For one thousand years or more, pilgrims have walked the Camino visiting the shrine of St. James, fabled for holding a relic of the great Saint.

At this news, Henrietta beamed, intuitively knowing this was what her dream had been about, and she immediately made plans to embark on the pilgrimage which, in turn, gave her the impetus to review why her past three years had been so chaotic. Courageously and with Sandalphon's help, she steadfastly brought her emotional body back into alignment, particularly in regard to the issues of anger and blame, and at last her soul became more integrated within her body, whilst the amber light around her became stronger and stronger.

That night, I had an intense dream of an Amber Orb protecting Henrietta as she cheerfully walked a long road, and upon which she had three remarkable encounters: one was in relation to a bronze chest, which was covered with beautiful amber stones and, on opening the box, Henrietta found the word Evolution written on old parchment; the second was at a gnarled tree which had been hit by lightning, some of which had struck sand near the tree, turning the sand into a crystal formation, like glass; the third was meeting a very old woman who pointed determinedly to the ground with her finger.

There was no doubt in my mind that Sandalphon was bringing oracular information to Henrietta and, before she set forth on her Camino pilgrimage, I revealed the dream.

The first encounter held little mystery – this was a profound journey for her to take in 'evolution' of her process; the second signified that she would be hit by spiritual lightning, crystallizing a truth about her destiny, and that this would be clarified through her connection with the Earth providing transformation; thirdly, that Henrietta would reveal to herself (the older wise woman within her would step forth) an inner wisdom about her mature Anima, and that she would always be connected with the Earth.

Henrietta absorbed this information as she set forth on her sojourn, surrounded by the loving force of Sandalphon's energy, feeling aligned, healthy and clear about what she wished for her evolution.

This was many years ago; Henrietta now lives her destiny, fulfilling her vocation by working as a brilliant landscape gardener of some repute. Henrietta uses profound eco-friendly principles in her work, is happily married with three children, and is constantly devoted to Sandalphon's capacious force.

A Prayer to Angel Sandalphon

Use this prayer, or perhaps one of your own creations, and you will elicit Sandalphon's loving support. A small amount of practice, lovingly making a request of this beautiful Angel, will show immediate results. You will perceive these intuitively, whilst sensing a sudden resolution to a challenge, an intense feeling of being led more implicitly by the Universe, an immense awareness that you may give all to Divine will, an intimate reminder of your own sovereignty which has hardwired Guardianship within you, or an even more wondrous sense of how to just let go and surrender to the Angels. All and more is possible!

Dear Archangel Sandalphon,
Thank you for blessing the world with your presence.
Thank you for bringing Angelic grace to the world of nature, and to the elemental forces.
Please bring me the harmony of balanced accord, enlightening my service to creation, allowing me to put my trust in surrendering to the natural cycles of life.
Please allow me to connect with the vibration of balance between my material and spiritual life.
So be it.
Amen

A daily affirmation to draw in Sandalphon's force

May I be clear with my love
May I trust the power of evolution
May I respect the Earth's cycles
May I live in peace

A MEDITATION FOR BECOMING AT ONE WITH SANDALPHON'S PRESENCE

1. Find yourself in a sacred space, whether this be a natural landscape, or your meditation room

2. Light a candle, burn some Sandalwood (Sandalphon's scent or essence), and play ambient music to consecrate the space with pure, loving intention

3. Having consecrated the space, breathe in and out your intention to be in the presence of Sandalphon throughout the space and. if you possess a piece of Amber, hold it in your hand or, if lying down, place it on your heart

4. Align your spine, and create a Mudra by placing your thumb and forefinger together. Feel your whole presence vigilant whether you are sitting or lying down

5. Breathe deeply with the breath-light moving through your whole being. Feel SILENCE, SOLITUDE AND STILLNESS, for the latter will nourish your soul

6. Breathe deeply and sound *OM* through your heart chakra seven times; this will draw Sandalphon's presence into your energy field

7. Rest and notice how pure force extends from your heart into the space before you, by seven feet (2m). As your force intensifies, imagine a beautiful Amber/Brown Orb ray of light emerging from the ending of your heart's ray. This is the force of the Angel Sandalphon's presence. Then rest and listen to the Oracular whisperings of this Angel's magical presence full of love, empathy and clarity. As you meditate, you will feel the supernal light of the seventh dimensional energies of the Archangelic kingdoms loving you and healing you by the sacred Communion with the Angels of Atlantis.

Namaste

SHAMAEL

DIVINE GUIDE

"The glory of the guide inspires us
to find love without seeking."

NINE

ANGEL SHAMAEL

Archangel Shamael has flowed as an exquisite Lilac Orb Ray through the vastness of the Cosmos since before time as we know it. Shamael administers to the core principles of life on the Earth, enfolding the very fabric of humanity with a perpetual guiding love, as well as blessing the diverse flora and fauna of this domain with equal beneficence.

Shamael, often written as Chamuel or Samael, exudes loving clarity and celestial guidance about the Universal Law of Intention, as mentioned in the Prologue and, with this degree of enlightenment, ubiquitously assists the one who seeks God – for this exquisite Angel accompanies us all through our lives, like a beacon of hope that never ceases to wane or lose shimmering focus.

Jesus found this in the garden of Gethsemane during his darkest night, when Shamael provided the assurance of love, as well as powerful information concerning his resurrection. The vast love of this great Angel created a ray of hope that overshadowed the burden of the mortal flesh, a ray made of light that shone so brightly that it guided Jesus through his vast dilemma by gently alleviating the shafts of pain with the pure love of heaven.

Likewise for us, Shamael's force is significant, loving and wise during times of colossal change such as bereavement, disease, divorce, or when resignation or redundancy occurs at work. When we are smitten by a test such as death, if we truly ask Shamael on bended knee for guidance, this loving Angel always brings forth succour and guidance concerning which path we should take – the path that fulfills the glory of our divine inheritance.

You see, the love Shamael offers is the love that transcends and transmutes the ordinary self. This love moves our consciousness through the wastelands of despair into the depths of a balm of compassion such that we arrive in the sanctuary of emotional maturity. Thus, this Angel removes from us the superfluities of life, striking the cosmic note of serenity in our hearts and souls, thence we meet the light of a new beginning, and we release attachment to the sentimentality of the past. And so we are deeply nourished, and inspired to remove from of our lives those aspects that diminish our belief in the Divine and all that is sacred. Thus, through aeons of time, this Divine Guide has been seen as the Angel most associated with the substance of creative evolution, for love is the igniting force for the joy of creation. If we openly love with the deep passion of our hearts, all that is associated with our métier reveals itself and manifests riches beyond compare.

Moreover, Shamael governs the SOUL STAR Chakra in human beings, helping us to draw our souls gently into our bodies whilst we heal the personal and collective trauma of our past. This soul-filled heart healing then anoints us with the divine compassion of our incarnation, and we bask in the balm of beatific bliss.

Communion of Guides

In Atlantis, all living beings were aware of their Soul Star, and the reason for incarnating on Planet Earth. This clarity of intention amplified the Christos energy on the planet, allowing the feminine aspect of the Earth Mother to shine forth, radiant with peace and love. This sustained the work of the communion of GUIDES, who were governed by the great High Priestess MAAT.

This remarkable being, assisted by Shamael, reckoned the force of truth in Atlantis. Indeed, later in ancient Egypt, Maat was given responsibility for the final judgment of human souls as they passed at the point of death into the Halls of Truth.

In Atlantis as in Egypt, the heart was a symbol for the seat of the soul, and therefore was hallowed as a giver and receiver of life. To live truthfully, honestly and with goodness meant that the individual's soul was 'light-hearted'. In the death rituals of Ancient Egypt, the heart was the only organ left within the body during the embalming process, with the other internal organs being removed for preservation in canopic jars. The reason for this was that the heart was considered to be quintessential for the sustainment of life after death – the heart was the holistic representation of the person's entire character or being.

High Priestess Maat

Maat's existence in Egypt was closely associated with Ra, whom she was considered to be the daughter of, and was known as the consort of Thoth. On an Angelic level, this brought Shamael's assistance of the GUIDES communion into closer vibration with Gabriel (the Messenger) and Uriel (the Companion), illustrating how inter-connected the presence of the twelve Angels was in Atlantis, just as they are today.

Ask yourself how you may draw Shamael's force closer to your life process, and deep into your own heart. The questions below will help to magnetize Shamael's existence into your heart, allowing angelic bliss to move fully within your body's cells. Therefore, when you petition and praise Shamael, the force of this wonderful Guide will automatically call you to great clarity of purpose, and so be prepared: your life will be transformed!

1. Am I open to the wisdom of uncertainty and the possibility of change?
2. Do I believe in the liberation of new beginnings, or am I held by fear of change?
3. Does my heart, as the seat of the soul, feel itself to be alight with life?
4. Am I allowing serenity within to meet each of my days?
5. Do I seek the truthful countenance of others?
6. Which of my body chakras opens me to Shamael's supreme guidance?
7. When do I bring awareness of the Angel's elixir into my day?
8. Do I allow my heart to guide me through life?
9. Is my life oriented by truth, goodness and love?
10. Does my consciousness open to the compassion of myself, and of the world?
11. What levels of elevated thought and feeling can I bring to my day of life-love?
12. Do I enjoy cultivating the divine aspect of my human self?

Asking these questions of yourself, and others that you may perceive through your own intuitive intelligence, will allow answers to be fermented deep within your soul. In turn, this will bring Shamael's energy closer to you. As a consequence, you will experience an exquisite stillness deep within you, allowing true guidance to impact on the major decisions of your life. If not, practice healing techniques with a trusted practitioner to help move you from the toxicity that mars perception. Try to remove the negativity that seizes the preternatural sense of your life and stifles your sensitivity to receive Angelic guidance. The Angels of Atlantis resonate with the highest good, the most celestial love.

No pessimist ever discovered the secrets of the stars, or sailed to uncharted land, or opened a new heaven to the human spirit. All are welcome, and yet all must open to the gentle benefaction of love!

– HELEN KELLER

The most salient resonance is that Shamael's vibration and presence will draw you to the inner counsel of your soul so that your own light's refraction, indeed your whole essence, will guide you through the moments of life's mighty impact when all else seems to fall away. These are the moments when we must fervently listen to the inner pulsations of our soul. This is when we are truly moved by the power of truth and honesty, to carve out our own grace in the annals of the world. This is when we fulfill our incarnation by claiming each aspect of life back into the expression of our divinity. This is when the extraordinary mystery of life suddenly receives a ray of light that catches our breath, and disturbs our rational mind, even bringing forth a tear, so that more love seeps into us, and we realize nothing will be the same again.

So, dear one, do record these moments of epiphany!

———

Maat's presence as an archetype will also help. Indeed, drawing Shamael closer to you by the use of the Icon that heads this chapter will move you closer to the reminder that divine order will prevail regardless of human whim or personal drama.

Our nature as humans is to look for balance and, as feeling is the language of the soul, true spiritual justice is always present, even if the world appears to be unfair and sullied. For, you see, divine justice is based on love, fairness and deep acceptance, and these three tenets are formulated through the ability to let go, to yield, to cascade into surrender. Then, when we have let go, in a moment of calm, the natural order of the universe lifts us towards our highest and most complete joy, liberating us from our fears and self-imposed limitation.

If we resist divine will, we create frustration, struggle and hardship. But, once we let go of fear, divine order springs in, and we are moved through challenge to compassion, then mercy, and are given Angelic support. In this we learn true guidance, for true compassion is borne of true objectivity, and so we finally realize the heart is not a sentimental organ, but one that is truthful, brave, august, fine, and deeply knowing.

The heart, as the seat of the soul, reverberates with wisdom when we become honest with our love, as we release ourselves from resentment, rejection and regret using the balm of forgiveness. Whether this be through releasing self-blame, or releasing the blaming of others – when dispensed with, we take our rightful place in the great scheme of things. The past is over, it has become history; the future calls and yet is unwritten, and the present claims us for infinite salvation.

You see, in this truth, there is no more than the moment, and this moment, and this moment.

Hades

In ancient Greece, Maat's archetypal force was appointed to the character of the God HADES, and in Rome Pluto. These were the Gods of the Underworld, the expanded realm of the individual or collective soul, the vast region of the unconscious. Indeed, it was once believed in the great Eleusinian mystery schools of ancient Greece that the major challenges of life experienced by the Initiate – meaning those experiences of the long dark night of the soul, those steeped in madness, depression, and near-death experiences – were descents into the underworld, the realm of Hades. Once these journeys had been made, there was no longer any fear of death.

Interestingly, there is an extraordinary story that concerns Hades, which may explain the sudden or catastrophic climate change that took place just prior to the death of Atlantis.

During many of the pinnacle years of expansion in Atlantis, the sacred intention of the Priests and Priestesses created the scientific technology that in turn created a biosphere, which was a safeguard for life on the planet. This etheric dome of vast proportion protected the souls that lived in the twelve communions of the continent. Effectively, life was protected from the ravaging galactic storms and solar flares that took place in the 'overworld' at that time, when unique weather conditions were brought about by the scientific experiments performed, which changed the energy grid of the planet, but did not affect the dedication, faith and ritual zeal of the people.

Another story about Hades concerns his 'rape' of Persephone, the daughter of Demeter, the Goddess of the Grain and the nurturing Mother of All. Hades desired Persephone for his bride, and with the consent of Father Zeus, abducted the maid into the underworld. The story proceeds that Persephone languished in the underworld for some time, whilst her mother grieved and raged at a loss so great that she withdrew into her Temple. Therefore, no crops grew, no births occurred, and no new life was brought forth. Indeed, famine so threatened the Earth with devastation that Zeus relinquished his control, sending Hermes into the underworld to rescue and heal the lass.

Hermes discovered the disconsolate Persephone in the clutch of Hades and persuaded him to let her go. But before Persephone was released, Hades gave her pomegranate seeds to eat, which meant that she was obligated to spend part of the year – the winter months when the Earth lies fallow – in the underworld alongside him. Thus, Persephone became the Queen of the Underworld, albeit for part of the year she was allowed to be in the mortal plane.

So began the deeper vibrational descent from the higher spiritual dimensions of Atlantean life, which grossly affected all inhabitants of the continent. However, Shamael, in loving iridescent Lilac form, continued to serve, support, and nurture the communion of the GUIDES who moved under the instruction of Maat to an area west of Atlantis. This we now know as the Yucatan peninsula, although in 10,000 BC the land mass inevitably appeared rather different from today.

There, the large city of Palenque grew, created by the Maya peoples as descendents of the Atlanteans, and associated with the ritual worship of the seasons. This area of land was rich in a fertile soil and an increase of plant life, which fostered the lifestyle of the early colonists who particularly enjoyed the coconut plant, drinking its juice, which was rich with almost three hundred phyto-nutrients. Similarly, these people enjoyed the luscious humidity, which fed their skin with the elixir of water, and so produced great health.

The GUIDES communion on Atlantis espoused the values that were fostered by Maat:

1. A sacred bond with the truth and simplicity of LOVE
2. A constant respect for the health and vitality of one's body as a reflection of the Earth
3. A love and honouring of the soul as a spectrum for the divine in human form
4. A diligence and zeal to function from the highest calling, therefore dispelling confusion
5. An upholding of the notions of truth and goodness
6. A deep recognition for the sacredness of life in sacred and profane form
7. An intense regard for the vibration of love transcending all things

8. A profound awareness of how the subtleties of nature govern with peace
9. The ability to stretch one's consciousness by surrendering all aspects of personal gain
10. The capability of developing the natural senses as beacons of guidance, to be used through the terrain of life
11. A veneration of the eternal jewels of love and joy as priorities
12. The ability to dispel fear by remaining in the sanctity of each moment, and using the LILAC RAY to cultivate grace and equilibrium

An Angel Shamael Story

Lisa was an actress of some repute who sought my guidance concerning a very significant life choice she needed to make. Lisa's very full career had been placed on hold during the time of an intense personal relationship which culminated in her becoming pregnant, and now another transition needed to occur.

However, two and a half years prior to this meeting, I had consulted with Lisa for an immersion in Angelic Sound Healing. Her story was that although happily preoccupied with a fascinating career, she also deeply desired a stable relationship with a loving man, and the experience of becoming a Mother – in a sense, to fulfill her creative destiny as a priestess of Aphrodite, for Lisa is a beauty!

Although both desires did not appear to be manifesting, Lisa was determined to create both through the powerful universal law of attraction, and so diligently practiced her daily meditations, affirmations and 'feeling good' processes, which had brought about rich creative manifestation before, in the form of great work opportunities.

In fact, I was truly impressed by Lisa's ability to manifest, and so was slightly surprised by her seeming impatience and lack of faith. However, believing in the force of Divine Will as I do, full support was given to Lisa, and I requested that she amplify her creative process. This she did by drawing in the heavenly guidance of Archangel Shamael.

I could see clearly that Angel Shamael had been very close to Lisa for some time, accompanying her whenever thoughts and feelings were jettisoned into space as rockets of desire. For whenever Lisa engaged in her manifestation process, her passion and zeal made her aura shine with a deep crimson force, particularly around her lower body. On these occasions, I was also aware of the powerful Lilac Ray of Shamael the Divine Guide, circling her Ajna Chakra, the vestigial third eye. This allowed Lisa to acquire the most beautiful Aura.

Lisa's quest was simple, knowing her positive energy would create with great aplomb. Then something delightful happened – it was her fortieth birthday, and she decided to have a party. Having eschewed the notion in earlier years, Lisa's preparations were exotic – choosing the right venue, investigating the best menu, organizing florists, and whatever best Champagne could be served as liquid refreshment – fine detail was the order of the day!

When her birthday came, Lisa looked radiant and I was happy to experience what truly became a joyous party. Everywhere I looked, I saw Shamael's Lilac Ray, and just knew that something miraculous was about to take place, at which point, in walked a handsome man whom Lisa had not known before. He had heard the sounds of the party, it being held in the reception room of an exclusive London hotel, and had decided to investigate the joy. Lisa was immediately drawn to this handsome Frenchman and, after the party, they exchanged telephone numbers, and then began dating. Shamael had literally guided François to the party, even to the point of wearing a Lilac shirt!

Ten months into their relationship, Lisa contacted me to inform me that she was pregnant and that she was about to take a one year sabbatical from her itinerant work as an actress, as she felt she was guided by the divine counsel of Angel Shamael.

———————

When we re-met post pregnancy, when Lisa was well into mother-hood, it was wonderful to see that she had expanded her contact with the Angelic kingdom, and that she felt illumined by the love offered for her next creative project. She simply needed an injection from me to help her inch her way forward to the fulfillment of her desire. In these moments, I was so aware of Lisa's insatiable curiosity and passion for life. Her fire made her sure that "the main thing was to keep the main thing, the main thing" – a powerful moral for all of us if we wish to develop our creative dreams.

Below is a prayer I exchanged with Lisa, and which may prove useful to you for your own creation.

A prayer to Angel Shamael

Dear Archangel Shamael,

Please help me to fully comprehend the teaching of change and the wisdom of uncertainty, particularly when I am tested by the change of my life.

Please let me see how adversity leads to abundance, and show me how wisdom shines when chaos leads to coherence.

Please direct me to administer my affairs through the true path of love so that I may not become caught by the illusions of the material world, and so that divine fulfillment resonates through each moment's breath, and helps me to my heart's desire

So be it.

Amen

A daily affirmation to draw in Shamael's force

May I be serene
May I trust my beginnings
May I love my curiosity
May I live in peace

A meditation for becoming at one with Shamael's presence

1. Find yourself in a sacred space, whether this be a natural landscape, or your meditation room
2. Light a candle, burn some Hyacinth (Shamael's scent or essence), and play ambient music to consecrate the space with pure, loving intentions
3. Having consecrated the space, breathe in and out your intention to be in the presence of Shamael throughout the space and, if you possess a Mother of Pearl, hold it in your hand or, if lying down, place it on your heart
4. Align your spine, and create a Mudra by placing your thumb and forefinger together. Feel your whole presence vigilant whether you are sitting or lying down

5. Breathe deeply with the LILAC Orb breath-light moving through your whole being. Feel SILENCE, SOLITUDE AND STILLNESS, for the latter will nourish your soul

6. Breathe deeply and sound *OM* through your heart chakra seven times; this will draw Shamael's presence into your energy field

7. Rest and notice how pure force extends from your heart into the space before you, by seven feet (2m). As your force intensifies, imagine a beautiful LILAC ray of light emerging from the ending of your heart's ray. This is the force of the Angel Shamael's presence. Then rest and listen to the Oracular whisperings of this Angel's magical presence full of love, serenity and initiative. As you meditate, you will feel the supernal light of the seventh dimensional energies of the Archangelic kingdoms loving you and healing you by the sacred Communion with the Angels of Atlantis

Namaste

"The treasure within the infinite depth of your soul
is your greatest friend."

TEN

ANGEL URIEL

Uriel is associated with numerous fables and legends in which the identity of this Angelic Orb has morphed into a multitude of different forms and characteristics. For Uriel's status has always been regarded as protean, whilst performing feats of such magnitude.

The names that have been attributed to Uriel are the 'Fire of God'; the 'Angel of the Presence'; the 'Flame of God'; the 'Regent of the Sun'; the 'Archangel of Salvation'; the 'Heavenly Interpreter'; and the 'Prince of Truth and Knowledge'. Literally, the nomenclature goes on and on.

Uriel is the Angel that stood at the gate of the Garden of Eden with the sword of fire, as a Cherubim; Uriel was responsible for burying the body of Adam in Paradise; Uriel was appointed the companion of Noah, and is the first being to have told him of the impending deluge; Uriel was given the Book of the Cabbala as a gift to Man; Uriel was the Magi of Alchemy who gave this proto-science to the great Chemists as a gift to mankind. And further still, Uriel's list of appointments was so rich with significance that this Angel became known as "one of the immortal Angels that companioned the undying God".

The pink Orb of Uriel represents the union of Heaven and Earth, made manifest through the beauty of the human heart. It is the fruit of the marriage between the physical heralding of the red ray, and the divine awakening of the white ray. In this form, the pink ray cascading forth represents unconditional love. It is the magic of the love we may offer another – an act of pure giving free of self-interest. It is the love that transforms and transcends the self, moving us through compassion towards a state of spiritual maturity. This is the incandescent love that is rich with 'charisma', for he or she who possesses this power will be faithful to the notion of a completely open heart. These are they who are warm and friendly to others, using reassurance, calmness, empathy, and uplifting inspiration, to touch the hearts of the collective.

Abundance, freedom, friendship, compassion and trust are their watch words, abiding love is their compass.

This exquisite angelic force can also be known as Ouriel, Auriel or Oriel and, as the angel of destiny, this divine companion fully knows the secrets of our incarnation through the folds of time-past and time-future. Indeed, as a companion, Uriel maintains a powerful link with the knowledge of our life's journey, shining light on our path as we stumble forward, helping us to call our soul back into our bodies if we choose to let it leave – through adversity, ill-health, or intemperance.

Communion of the Companions

Therefore, in Atlantis, Uriel governed the Communion of the COMPANIONS assisting the High Priest Ra Horus, whose visionary energy was wrought through the faculties of prophecy, art and beauty. Horus's symbol in Atlantis was the illustrious figure of eight, the symbol of infinity, which illustrated Horus's abilities to perceive the inner-folds of creation and the landscape of the perpetual, indicating the sacredness of life as an experience eternal!

Later, in Egypt, Horus was believed to be the son of Osiris and Isis, and therefore held an eminent position, being equally identified with the Sun and majesty of the Priest Kings – the Pharaohs. Horus's symbol was the divine falcon whose all-seeing eye represented clairvoyance, heightened vision and cosmic awareness.

Likewise, the Atlantean Temple of the Companions was a sanctuary for prophecy, where rituals were established to awaken the all-seeing eye of clairvoyance. Of the twelve Temples in each of the communions, this was one of the most beautiful – again circular in design, reflecting the nature of the inclusivity of companionship, which is 'all one'. The temple was painted white, pink and cobalt blue, with Rose, Clear and Seriphos Green Quartz, accompanied by Moonstones and Opals, used to synbolize the unique marriage between Heaven and Earth. The pink of Rose Quartz amplified the worshippers' alignment with the nature of the universal and cosmic heart chakra.

Archangel Uriel overshadows the eighth Chakra of the Universal Heart (whereas Zadkiel overshadows the tenth Cosmic Heart Chakra), connecting the individual with the notion of universal love – that within the Universe all living beings are one interconnected force, so giving rise to companionship. For the Universal Heart Chakra is the route through which the soul awakens the mental body of the person, illuminating the conviction of the fact that "what is above, is also below" and therefore clarifying the power of spiritual discernment.

Through this Chakra, objectivity awakens, bringing detachment from the conditioned beliefs that no longer feel real within the perspective of living our lives as spiritual beings on a human journey. Further still, through the UNIVERSAL HEART, we receive oracular messages from the spiritual realms, which download into the seven personal chakras of the physical, emotional and mental bodies.

The Atlanteans steadfastly ritualized their connection with the universe through this chakra, for it was the vector of force that constantly moved them to the conviction of the non-local reality of their love – that love is all there is; that love is the exquisite consciousness of all that exists, and so evokes companionship as a core ingredient within the Cosmos.

Ask yourself how you may draw Uriel's force closer to your own heart. The questions below will help to magnetize Uriel's existence in your life experience, and ultimately in your soul. The quest here is to allow this Angelic presence to move fully within your body's cells, so that grace and truth are truly made flesh. Therefore, when you petition Uriel, the force of this wonderful Companion will automatically call you to the purpose of love, and your life will be transformed forever:

1. Is my heart open to love?
2. Is my life a pathway for companionship?
3. What aspects of my being guide my loving?
4. Do I feel that my love can open the doorway of my intuition?
5. The love referred to here is not 'sentimental': can you perceive the difference?
6. Whom do I see in my community, or the world, as an example of this love?
7. Do I engage in an act of compassion every day?
8. How often do I engage in my foresight, my clairvoyance?
9. Have I developed the power of inner vision in companionship?
10. Do I choose who I break bread with (in other words: enjoy a meal with)?
11. Do I perceive the interconnectedness of all life?
12. What would I specifically like Uriel to bring me?

Dutifully study this quest, requesting deep feelings to emerge from your inner core, and allowing the answers to seep into your soul's very fabric. As a consequence, you will experience beautiful serenity immersed within your being, allowing true guidance to impact on the major decisions of your life.

If not, practice healing techniques with a trusted practitioner to help move you from the physical and emotional toxicity that mars your perception. Try to release the force that seizes the preternatural sense of your life, that stifles your sensitivity from receiving Angelic guidance. The faith produced by Uriel will inevitably help because it resonates with the highest good, the most celestial love.

The more we dwell in the power of the Angelic kingdom, the more we meditate on their exquisite energies, the more we beseech Angelic aid – the more we feel their ultimate effect in our lives. For all we need remember is that their loving power has a ubiquitous frequency, and our personal vibration has become unused to receiving this refined transmission. Therefore, regularly tune into meditation, practice chant and prayer, and you will feel yourself becoming more easily connected with the intuitive super highway where the Angels roam.

During the colonization of Egypt, and after the deluge that drew Atlantis to its watery grave, Ra Horus took the communion of the COMPANIONS to Greece, where they seeded a civilization that became, as we know, greatly influential in the development of the western world. Although this colonization occurred long before the Archaic Period of the early eighth century BC, when established history suggests ancient Greece was formed.

High Priest Ra Horus and Apollo

In the early history of Greece, a mythology arose that transformed the High Priest Ra Horus into the personality of Apollo, or Phoebus in Roman lore. Apollo ranked second only to Zeus, as the foremost of the Greek Gods, for Apollo was the God of the Sun, of Prophecy, of the Arts and Music, and was celebrated for his pure and cleansing nature. Indeed, a symbol of the Sun was used to represent his being for, like Ra Horus, he appeared not just to have been born of the sun but to be a supernal radiation of its presence, and so the sun overshadowed the evocation of this divine being.

Like the sacred Temple of Ra Horus in Atlantis, the worship of Apollo inspired the famous Temple at Delphi. Delphi was considered to be the womb of the Earth, the centre or Omphalos of the known world, and the very nexus of all things sacred; the Temple was constructed over a fissure rent in the Earth.

As you entered the Temple, one would see inscribed on the lintel above the door: *Know Thyself: To Thine own-self be true*, and within the deeper halls of this extraordinary sanctuary, the great Sibyls performed their famous oracular powers with outstanding perspicacity. Interestingly, Apollo's Oracles were all women, and an exegete or priest-interpreter would attend the Priestesses. When they spoke, as for example when Pythia, known as the most famous Oracle, uttered her Paeans of exaltation, the priest would record and interpret her sayings. Therefore, people came to the Temple for two major reasons, in addition to the deification of Apollo himself: they came to consult the oracle for life direction, and to obtain healing purification for crimes that had been committed.

From an archetypal perspective, Apollo represented that aspect of being which yearns for the Solar Logos: the light of the world from which we receive healing, optimum illumination, forgiveness, wisdom and ultimate enlightenment. Through worship of Apollo, people connected with the divine through the beauty of art and music, for Apollo was the patron of music and poetry. Indeed, it is recorded in the ancient legends that he led the divine Muses and their supernal choir, to heal through music and harmony – both of which are closely aligned with work of the Angels. This is the reason why they have chosen the symbol of the great OM in the Icon that appears at the beginning of this chapter.

Hermes (whose identity was linked with Thoth) gave Apollo a remarkable Lyre which was believed to have magical properties, and which healed human beings and nature alike. Therefore, Apollo was considered the God of Medicine and Healing, the power of which he dispensed to his son Asclepius.

Archangel Uriel identifies Asclepius with the supreme healing medicines, and Asclepius' daughters: Hygieia meaning 'Hygiene', Iaso meaning 'Medicine', Aceso meaning 'Health', and Panacea meaning 'Universal Remedy' were further extensions of this powerful healing and offered in the remarkable Temples of Asclepius. Indeed, the rod of Asclepius and Hermes, a snake-entwined staff or caduceus, remains the archetypal symbol of medicine to this day.

The COMPANIONS communion on Atlantis espoused these values, which were also fostered by Ra Horus:

1. A sacred bond with the interconnectivity of life, and conscious creation through friendship
2. A respect for the healing, harmony and happiness of self and others
3. An honouring of feeling as the language of the soul
4. A total belief in the abundance of the Universe

5. An upholding of the virtues of honour and trust
6. A deep recognition of the sacredness of companionship
7. An utter belief in the rite of freedom for all
8. A profound awareness of how love is all there is, permeating the very folds of creation
9. The ability to stretch one's consciousness by surrendering personal ambition to collective aspiration
10. A constant recognition of the landscape without as a mirror of the landscape within. Therefore, realizing there is no blame, only insight
11. A veneration of the eternal jewels of grace and love in friendship
12. The contemplation of beauty in all things, so as to establish Divine order through creation

AN ANGEL URIEL STORY

An Apollo-like figure came to my practice a few years ago. Jack was a light-filled sixteen-year-old Indigo/Crystal child that had attended one of my Angelic Sound Healing workshops in London. Jack had found conventional schooling extremely challenging – he had been identified as dyslexic, and yet his ability to see through the pain and chaos of those people who led the educational cultures he was part of gave him a penetrative quality far beyond his youth, which unsettled many of those around him.

Jack was a walking emotional barometer; an empath with exacting psychic awareness, who literally internalized the kaleidoscope of feeling states experienced by the person beside him. Instantaneously, Jack could provide a reading of the individual, which mostly proved to be an accurate scan of their inner landscape. This included seeing with X-Ray eyes which body organ was affected and, in so doing, he took the energy of the person into his own being in order to transform it. Jack had come to the series of workshops to discover methods of delineation, detachment, a clearer Mediumship, and a greater protection in service to the all that is.

The Indigo beings started arriving on Planet Earth in the middle part of the Eighteenth Century – Mozart was an Indigo – and they have extraordinary abilities of leadership, feeling that they are heaven-sent to either gift the culture into which they are born with remarkable creativity, or with the ability to champion a certain cause. Their role is to penetrate established order and to change any systems that lack integrity and, for this, they are often borne with warrior spirits: fiery, zealous and extremely passionate. Indigos often have alternative learning abilities, finding conventional education principles, based on left brain acuity very challenging, for their right brain creative/intuitive processes dominate their consciousness.

The Crystal Children began to appear on the planet during the later part of the twentieth century, although some arrived earlier. These beings are extremely powerful, their main purpose is to take us to the next level of evolution, to reveal to us our inner divinity. They function as a group consciousness rather than as individuals, and they live by the "Law of One" – the Christos Unity Consciousness. They are powerfully telepathic and hold the force of love and peace on the planet, with fully awakened eight Chakras.

Jack had shown the basic abilities for literacy and numeracy much later than his peers, not because of possessing a low IQ, but because of perceiving 'reality' from a different perspective. As a result of this sensibility, Jack felt at odds with most people, societies and ways of being, including his own family.

This led me to understand that Jack was a STAR CHILD, who hadn't as yet identified his planetary home.

Jack had moved through the early stages of Secondary School, where his soul found it difficult to interface with the peer pressure of the school environment, the academic competition, educational streaming and examination orientation. He confessed to not feeling superior, just profoundly different, and that he felt the lack of collaboration to be absurd; he wanted to transform the substance of competition into the art of collaboration, and had devised a method of changing the face of established politics. Fairness, rightness, love, truth, goodness and grace were his major preoccupations and, often not seeing reflections of these jewels in the world, he had become involved in activities that made him conscious-less; by drinking alcohol, taking drugs, and behaving outrageously – he had even taken his Mother's car to 'joy-ride' one evening before passing his driving test, and had crashed the vehicle, fortunately without hurting himself or anyone else.

Jack felt isolated and awkward about developing friendships with other adolescents of his age, preferring to be with 'older' people, whose conversation he admired. Jack actively sought out people of a higher calibre and had bravely attended a number of spiritual groups in London, endeavouring to establish contact with spiritual richness, and to create a vibrational match with someone of similar propensities. On one occasion, he had also felt sexually attracted to another young man of similar age, and yet found it extremely difficult to articulate his feelings. Although Jack could intuitively understand this behaviour, he felt isolated, not knowing how to create physical or emotional contact with others. At this tender age, he simply hadn't processed the knowing that time brings: it is through the experience of earthing that maturity may shine a light on the path of life.

We set out a strategic plan to draw kindred spirits into his life, those whom he felt in empathy with. This consisted of a pragmatic list:

1. Whom did he wish to meet?
2. What their interests would be?
3. What their social background would be?
4. How emotionally intelligent they would be?
5. How conscious of their spiritual initiation they would be?
6. What the purpose of the meeting would be – for fun, shared interests, kindred spirit, dating?
7. What advantages would there be?
8. What disadvantages would there be?
9. Would this *feel good* and would the individual have integrity?
10. How to protect against leaking force?
11. What the soul guidance of the situation would be?
12. Where the soul being had originated?

Whilst clarifying this process, and perceiving the many levels of Jack's vibrational frequency, I was also aware that he was surrounded by spirits, both in terms of his family guardian spirits, and the august spiritual lineage from which his soul derived vast wisdom – some of whom were of extra-terrestrial origin, associated with the intergalactic counsel.

Uriel's Pink Ray benignly over-shadowed this sacred enclave, and I encouraged Jack to bring this exquisite Angelic companion into his daily meditations, both as petitioning and receiving stances. In so doing, Jack found his meditation practice deepened and great stillness started to occur, drawing Uriel's magic forth to shine more thoroughly. Often Jack would smell the essence of rosemary, Uriel's unique calling card and the vibrational force that resonates the Angel's elixir in 3D.

Interestingly, during these times of deep contemplation, magic occurred in a number of ways to help Jack with his process, one being the manifestation of a wonderful nutritionist called Ariel (another of Uriel's names), who, through muscle-testing sequences, was able to discover what foods and liquids Jack was allergic to. This radically changed Jack's entire regime as it was discovered that wheat, sugar, dairy, coffee and tea were substances that brought out allergic reactions which had grossly disturbed his health.

Contemporary research shows that the food we eat substantially affects our consciousness and that, as we develop through the great shifts of force taking place within our Galaxy, we are similarly developing more sensitivity to the bio-chemical entirety of our lives. Without a shadow of a doubt, Indigo and Crystal beings experience major mood changes if they are exposed to genetically modified foods, or those foods that are not of the greatest purity. These swings of mood often result in hyper-activity.

Uriel's mineral stone is Pink Quartz, and so wearing a piece of quartz over the heart chakra also helped to modify Jack's abundant intake of stimuli, and at last he was beginning to feel more centred and harmonious.

Below is a prayer I recommended to Jack, and which may prove useful to you for bringing Uriel closer into your energy field.

A Prayer for Angel Uriel

Dear Archangel Uriel,

As you are placed in the role of a stabilizing presence here on Earth, please watch over me so that I may tread the path of gentleness and care.

Please teach me to be in the world and not of it, allowing my spiritual gifts to unfold, as well as bringing my material life to abundance.

I am destiny's child and so please show me the path of the greatest joy through which the way of love will be ultimately made manifest.

Therefore, please bring companions to join me on my path so that I may experience the joy of comrades.

So be it.

Amen

A DAILY AFFIRMATION TO DRAW URIEL'S FORCE

May I be abundant
May I constantly feel freedom
May I love my friendships
May I live in trust

A MEDITATION FOR BECOMING AT ONE WITH URIEL'S PRESENCE

1. Find yourself in a sacred space, whether this be a natural landscape, or your meditation room
2. Light a candle, burn some Rosemary (Uriel's scent or essence), and play ambient music to consecrate the space with pure, loving intention
3. Having consecrated the space, breathe your intention to be in the presence of Uriel throughout the space and, if you possess a piece of Pink Quartz, hold it in your hand or, if lying down, place it on your heart
4. Align your spine, and create a Mudra by placing your thumb and forefinger together. Feel your whole presence vigilant whether you are sitting or lying down
5. Breathe deeply with the PINK ray light moving through your whole being. Feel SILENCE, SOLITUDE AND STILLNESS, for the latter will nourish your soul
6. Breathe deeply and sound *OM* through your heart chakra seven times; this will draw Uriel's presence into your energy field
7. Rest and notice how pure force extends from your heart into the space before you by seven feet. As your force intensifies, imagine a beautiful PINK Orb ray of light emerging from the ending of your heart's ray. This is the force of the Angel Uriel's presence. Then rest and listen to the Oracular whisperings of this Angel's magical presence full of love, serenity and initiative. As you meditate, you will feel the supernal light of the seventh dimensional energies of the Archangelic kingdoms loving you and healing you by the sacred Communion with the Angels of Atlantis

Namaste

ZADKIEL

DIVINE COMFORTER

"Within the secret chamber of the heart
lives a mighty comforter."

ELEVEN

ANGEL ZADKIEL

Within the divine circle of the twelve Angels of Atlantis, Zadkiel represents the benign force of 'comfort', bestowed upon this celestial being by God to dispense through mercy, grace and benevolence.

This is the 'comfort' that fortifies our lives with a wealth of loving instruction concerning the power of our vulnerability, as well as our exquisite fragility. This is the vibration that conjures 'heart tingles' such as love, compassion, empathy, non-judgment, kindness, patience, sincerity, forgiveness and gratitude – to name just a few.

Through the quality of force created by this 'field of intention', Zadkiel protects and shields us from the demons, projections and fears of our own creation – for, make no mistake, it is we who pre-determine our anguish by disregarding the significance of our soul, our emotional intelligence, the knowledge that thought creates reality and that feeling actualizes creation. When we wake to the dawning freedom of this knowledge, we realize that there is nothing on earth that's good or bad, that it is thinking that makes it so – that being conscious means we see happiness as a decision, not as a condition.

When we vibrate thus, Zadkiel bestows beneficent wisdom upon us, allowing clear vision over any of the obstacles that are perpetuated by our own self-limiting patterns and beliefs, by those impediments that stop us from touching our own spiritual abundance. Zadkiel literally shows us what needs to be brought forth into the light and healed. Then, when fully identified and transmuted, we may open our hearts to divine grace, aspire to pure joy, and feel generosity and kindness pervading the world. Once, that is, we have healed the negativity by yielding it to Zadkiel's powerful ministrations.

Working with Zadkiel means a continuous flow of treasure, supported by the divine love that filters through and from this Angel, derived from the muscle of our own spiritual love, and actioned by belief, faith and trust. For, remember, the Source is a place of infinitely unfolding creative possibility full of love and joy. There is no scarcity, so budgeting your force isn't required, but only a belief in the splendour of loving creative action.

In this, Zadkiel reigns supreme, teaching us to trust in God's utter benevolence and guidance, for all we need do is let go and let God in, then the bounty of the Universe, indeed of the Source, becomes clear to us. Then the Source opens its heavenly gates to us, and we feel that there, in the unseen, everything is always spotlessly clean, all gadgets work, dust never settles, and all beings are as fit as a fiddle.

Zadkiel, or Hesediel, Tzadqiel, Satqiel, and Zachiel, are the many recorded names of this one Angel. Zadkiel is revered within the rabbinical tradition for the vast compassion bestowed upon truly significant individuals. For example, it is suggested that Zadkiel is the Angel who stayed the hand of Abraham from slaughtering his son Isaac, and also held Adam with forgiveness after the dramatic move from innocence in the Garden of Eden.

Communion of Comforters

On Atlantis, Zadkiel's force, as an emanation of ultimate good, was placed in allegiance to the communion of the COMFORTERS, and to the High Priestess ISIS, who epitomized devotion to the cause of the great Mother archetype, bestowing the force of her 'comfort' directly from the Galaxy.

The communion of the COMFORTERS assisted the vibrational work of other communions such as the HEALERS, by holding mercy and compassion as the lynchpins to their worship and service. This they did through constant ritual, worship and devotion; spending their time in meditative contemplation, and focusing on the inter-stellar energies that rained into the Temple – the central chamber of which became the sanctum sanctorum, containing extraordinary energies from the twelve planets of the galaxy. These energies were contained within the crystals placed in the sanctuary, in the living consciousness of Larimar, Amethyst, Quartz Crystal, Diamond, Aquamarine, Moon-stone, Opal, Tanzanite, Topaz, Rose Quartz, Lapiz Lazuli and Emerald: all gave their force to the amplification of the spiritual ideals.

The ideals and rituals of the COMFORTERS communion were dedicated to the promise of the Cosmic Heart Chakra (the tenth chakra positioned between the heart and throat) calibrated to be in harmony with the energy centres of the subtle and material body. The power of this chakra was dynamized by wearing collars of the sacred mineral Larimar; Larimar, or the Atlantis Stone, was used extensively in the dress of the Atlantean peoples, enabling an amplification of the higher frequency energies. The tenth chakra aligns the soul's incarnation with the interconnectedness of cosmic love. Thus, this communion helped to support and sustain many of the other sacred functions of the Atlantean continent, in a profound and comforting embrace.

───────────

To receive comfort by reading this chapter, gaze on the serene countenance of the icon that heads this chapter. Notice how the image of Mary, as the Divine Mother, looks heaven-wards, whilst the gaze of Jesus the Christ-child penetrates into your very being. The exquisite nature of the Christos – meaning 'the anointed one' – held the potential of the love-light circuitry within his flesh and subtle body. His Mother Mary was an initiated priestess of Isis, and the icon was chosen by the Angels of Atlantis to help you feel the implicit love of the Divine Mother drenching your consciousness. *How does it feel?*

Lovingly ask yourself how you may wish to draw Zadkiel's force deeper into your heart. The questions below will help to magnetize Zadkiel's existence into your life experience, and ultimately into your soul. The quest set here is to allow this Angelic presence to move infinitesimally through your body's cells, so that love, joy, gratitude and security are implicitly lodged within your flesh. Therefore, when you petition Zadkiel, the force of this wonderful Comforter will automatically call you to the purpose of your love, and in so doing, your life will be immediately transformed:

1. Is my heart open to the possibility and profundity of Cosmic Love?
2. Is my life a conduit of love, alleviating the suffering of others?
3. What part of me needs to be released before I accept Divine Love?
4. Is my heart, my universal heart, my cosmic heart, open to be a living crucible for the Cosmic Christ Love?
5. What feelings ,do I sense, summon the entirety of my heart's love?
6. How do I feel about other life forms within the Universe possessing similar, or perhaps more heightened love?
7. Will I seek comfort and the notion of FEELING GOOD in each action of each day?
8. Do I live in constant gratitude for the bounty and abundance of Planet Earth and the Universe?
9. Can I connect with the notion of SECURITY, or 'self-cure' to fill

my days?

10. May I see myself as a Starchild? If so, where am I from?
11. Do I allow myself to feel which planet I originally seeded from?
12. If my life were dedicated to the path of Zadkiel's love, what would I do and be with that loving energy?

Pondering these questions will bring inspiration, comfort, consolation and solace to the probability of your life as a light-being of the Universe in human form. As a consequence, you will experience a wondrous sensation deep within you coming from the Cosmos that will allow true supernal grace and guidance to impact on your major life decisions. If not, practice healing techniques with a trusted practitioner, to help move you from that which mars your ability to receive the loving pulsations of the Universe.

Attempt to release the force that seizes the loving pulsations and sensations of life, that holding point which stifles your sensitivity, and you will receive the Angelic guidance that resonates with the highest form of celestial love.

This is the quality of love that floods from the orb light frequency of Zadkiel's presence. This is the love that influenced the power of Isis, as an evocation of the divine Mother. Indeed, when the life of the Atlanteans altered considerably during the end times of their civilization, it was Isis who took the communion of the COMFORTERS and colonized the land we now know as Palestine, and they were responsible for creating the Essene Communities. One such community within this area brought forth Mary Magdalene, and the Mary who gave birth to the Jesus or Jeshua – both of these women were highly trained spiritual initiates, taking the role of Priestess to Isis, as they were anointed to perform.

The Essene community inhabited a settlement in the Judean Desert alongside the west bank of the Dead Sea which, in ancient times as today, was known as Qumran. These remarkable people were powerfully influenced by the Atlantean teachings, attempting to live their lives as channels of peace. What substantiated their faith was the strong influence of the ritual worship of Isis.

Isis and the Moon

Isis taught the Essene people the magic of her healing arts, largely derived from her direct communication, knowledge and worship of the Moon. This celestial orb has a gargantuan magnetic force which focuses on the bio-structure of Planet Earth (see the Prologue, how Planet Earth was once a living watery Orb itself, moving in conjunction with more than one moon), and therefore also upon human beings.

Our bodies comprise of eight-five percent water. This water element, mixed with the fluids of our bodies, and flowing through the liquid-scape of our whole being, is closely connected with our emotional body, and therefore with the vastness of our feelings. To this extent, it is a well-known fact that, if a group of women co-habit, their emotional energies become synchronized during the time of their monthly menstrual cycle, around the Full Moon.

Similarly, we may see the effect the moon has on the movement of Earth's oceanic tides, or the water crystals of our lives – as seen in Professor Masaru Emoto's work centred around the *Miracles of Water*. Emoto illustrates how thought-forms passing through frozen water produce outstanding geometrical patterns, clearly illustrating that thought creates reality, and that emotion actualizes thought. All and more allow us to see the moon is in governance of the planet's life tides and currents.

> *Therefore the Moon, the governess of floods,*
> *Pale in her anger, washes all the air,*
> *That rheumatic diseases do abound.*
> *And thorough this distemperature we see*
> *The seasons alter.*
>
> *– SHAKESPEARE*

Priestess Isis in Egypt

In ancient Egypt, Isis was known as the embodiment of the Divine Mother, just as Kali in Hinduism, Quan yin in Buddhism, or Mother Mary in Christianity were and are known to be of similar power. Egypt's ISIS was believed to be the daughter of the earth God Geb, and the sky goddess Nut, and sister-consort of Osiris, who jointly ruled with her, and so bestowed the munificence of the infinite ones in an unparalleled fashion upon the Earth.

Later, in ancient Greece and Rome, Isis took the guise of the Goddess Demeter (Greece) and Ceres (Rome) and, as such, they were similarly seen as the maternal archetype.

The mother archetype motivates us to nurture others through generosity and empathy, producing internal satisfaction for being the caretaker or caregiver. Thus the comforter, or nurturer aspect of the Demeter/Ceres archetype is expressed through the helping/healing professions – teaching, healing, counseling. Indeed, through any occupation that comforts and helps others, they are fundamentally part of this archetype.

Demeter was the most generous Goddess in the pantheon, as she gave humanity the hope of love, the passion for agricultural harvesting, the desire for material abundance, and the spiritual zeal of the Eleusinian Mystery Schools. Just so, many spiritual leaders have radiated Demeter's attributes: the saintly Mother Teresa of Calcutta; the woman referred to simply as "the Mother" in the role of the spiritual leader of the Sri Aurobindo Ashram; Mary Baker Eddy, who founded the Christian Scientist Church. Just so, each attribute signifies the divine nature of the Mother, firstly by taking care of physical needs, secondly by giving emotional support, and thirdly by leading through spiritual wisdom, so that the individual is comforted when diseased, alleviated when suffering, elevated from disappointment, and redirected when disoriented. Within these measures are secreted the meaning and mystery of life.

The COMFORTERS communion on Atlantis espoused these values, fostered by ISIS:

1. A sacred contract in the passion of nurturing and comforting those in travail
2. A respect for the healing arts, and the creation of divine harmony
3. An honouring that profound earthly magic creates the fulfillment of divine dreams
4. Respecting the Moon as a provider of magnetic love and of all the care that is needed
5. That the giver of solace, comfort and peace is recognizing the wellspring of infinity
6. Obeying a deep love for the comforting fabric of the universe and all the planets
7. An utter belief in the sacred force of Mother Nature as an aspect of the Divine
8. A profound awareness of how love is all there is, reverberating through the very sands of time
9. The ability to stretch one's heart to the full creation of happiness and joy
10. A constant yielding to the powerful guidance of the Divine Mother

11. A veneration of the eternal jewels of comfort and nurturance
12. A loyal meditation of the principles of Isis in the evocation of her harvesting nature

An Angel Zadkiel Story

The wonderment of life's mystery never ceases to send shivers of awe through me as I review the sacred majesty and earthy profanity of our lives, as I review the order and chaos, the light and dark, the vastness and minutiae, the sweet and sour, the hope and despair, the steadfast and bending, the courage and corruption, the noble and ignoble, the abundance and seeming lack, the concord and conflict, the ascending victory of love and the declining nature of the vainglorious: I recognize that all and more have been the contrasting sequence of our lives until, that is, this time of renaissance.

What makes me curious is that many of us rarely consider these degrees, unless we are pitched against one of life's bold and discerning moments: the days and nights that rack our ken, the moments that encourage us go deep inside, to attempt to find the most kind, the most resilient, the most wise, and the most loving comfort that exists within the fissures of that subterranean place of our unconscious. For, make no mistake, if we can journey thence, we reach the very promise and portal of our soul.

An alternative route is to review the jubilations of life, the dizzying heights of inspiration, the elevated moments of ascended joy as a pathway to the essence of all essence. Yet it seems we would rather choose desperation over inspiration to delve deep into the rifts and corries of our mind, in order to elicit change.

Zadkiel enters that place of our deeper consciousness via the channels of divine love. Bold, pervasive and firm in intent, this great COMFORTER brings us the deepest love, the greatest boon, and the fullest comfort ever. Often I find myself yearning, beseeching, sweetly seducing dear Zadkiel into arriving, in order to provide that Angelic-comfort that transmutes all pain – to assist the dear one who encounters the despair, death, pain, sorrow, or the utter bewilderment of psychic re-booting.

The great poets bring forth apprehension of this space. For example:

> *No worst, there is none: Pitched past pitch of grief,*
> *More pangs will, schooled at fore-pangs, wilder wring.*
> *Comforter, where, where is your comforting?*
> *Mary, mother of us, where is your relief?*
> *My cries heave, herds-long: huddle in a main, a chief*
> *Woe, world sorrow; on an age old anvil wince and sing,*
> *Then lull, then leave off. Fury had shrieked 'no lingering,*
> *Let me be fell: force I must be brief'*
> *O the mind, mind has mountains; cliffs of fall*
> *Frightful sheer, no-man fathomed.*

> *– GERARD MANLEY HOPKINS*

Words of this quality take us to those deep fissures, those spaces plumbed by great Poets/Artists because they also know. Perhaps they provide us with an explanation, as we are held in those moments when we face the dread chasm of fear, the bitter long dark night of the soul, the grave tragedy of death, or the searing bout with disease.

One such encounter I had with the raw edge of life and death was with Rogiero. He was sixty-two and had lived a life of compound stress which arose from the deep and subtle fear of having no self-worth. This fear had gripped him so tightly that he rarely expressed how he truly felt about the life he summoned into creation. This was heavy karma, and I first encountered him when he sought Sound Healing during a trial with cancer.

Rogiero had worked as a high calibre tailor on Saville Row (traditionally the home of bespoke tailoring in London, established over two hundred years), where he had been employed most of his adult life. Indeed, Rogiero was a superb craftsman with astonishing expertise, an intimate knowledge of fabrics and weave, and an uncanny sense – based on years of experience – of how to create a personalized cachet for the individual client; yet he constantly undermined and undervalued any of these unique qualities.

The hierarchy of the store where he toiled was extremely unjust, lacking emotional intelligence, perpetrating mis-creation and allowing conflicts to take place between co-workers, whatever their status or rank. Story after story emerged from Rogiero when he was with me, about the emotional brutality of his colleagues who were constantly vying for power, projecting personal spleen onto one another, engaging in emotional sabotage, and, it appeared, using this mild-mannered man as their 'whipping post'.

Rogiero constantly received 'the slings and arrows of outrageous fortune', so much so that my vision of Rogiero at work was of St. Sebastian, receiving arrow after arrow of unkind stripes. During the time of my meeting him, his body had had enough: he had suffered quietly for so long that now morphine nullified some of the despair, pain and conflict.

From the perspective of karma, powerful life choices were being made by Rogiero on deep levels of his soul, options drawn from prior lives when he had exerted cruelty and wretchedness on others. This Rogiero willingly accepted, and it was my privilege to support this dear one through the expiation of this karma, through the noble rite of atonement known as the Violet Flame.

However, during the last few weeks of his life, I was also fully aware, and in awe, of the constantly comforting support of a beautiful larimar-colored Orb hovering in presence with him. The light from the finely-tuned rays drenched Rogiero's energy field in sublime love, and much of his emotional pain, he commented, was quenched whilst at the same time being drawn to a sweeter, gentler, and more loving countenance. Thus Zadkiel's presence caressed his whole being with the sublime manna from heaven.

I respectfully drew on the force of this beautiful comforting Angel during these times with Rogiero, drawing the energy inexorably through me in order to positively charge Rogiero's extremely weakened energy field with the Chi of this bounty. Then, gently, one afternoon, he passed into spirit with peace, love and blessings escorting him into the finer dimensions of existence, all helped by Zadkiel. Afterwards I sat for a long time feeling the Larimar light of this Comforter Angel bathing my own being with a firmness of conviction, steadfastness and sweetness which released any attachment to the outcome of Rogiero's life, or my service to it.

If you are experiencing similar travail, please draw on this mighty comforting force and, with faith in Zadkiel's existence, you will also feel the light of the unvanquished ones filling your days and nights with peace, love and grace. And in order to focus the Angelic force through your life, please practice praise, petition and a sense of participation in the holy pact of meditation and prayer.

Praise and petition are accessed through chant and prayer (see the prayer below), whilst being aware that you are protected by the force of the enlightened ones in participation of a sacred act.

A Prayer to Angel Zadkiel

Dear Archangel Zadkiel,

Thank you for the comfort and abundance of Divine succour that you have revealed within me this day.

Thank you for bathing me in the rays of your deep, incandescent love, which shines from the deeper folds of heaven, drawing with it all the blessings of the Angels.

Please allow me to breathe the pure light of the immortal Pranayama, so that my vitality and strength may uplift the lives of my fellow lovers with God's light, love and joy.

And, as you journey through our lives, please awaken within us the glory of our gratitude for the gifts of spirit.

So be it.

Amen

A daily affirmation to draw Zadkiel's force

May I be grateful
May I constantly source security
May I love unendingly
May I live in trust

A meditation for becoming at one with Zadkiel's presence

1. Find yourself in a sacred space, whether this be a natural landscape, or your meditation room
2. Light a candle, burn some Sage (Zadkiel's scent or essence), and play ambient music to consecrate the space with pure, loving intention
3. Having consecrated the space, breathe in and out your intention to be in the presence of Zadkiel throughout the whole space and, if you possess a piece of Larimar, hold it in your hand or, if lying down, place it on your heart

4. Align your spine, and create a Mudra by placing your thumb and forefinger together. Feel your whole presence vigilant whether you are sitting or lying down

5. Breathe deeply with the breath-light moving through your whole being. Feel SILENCE, SOLITUDE AND STILLNESS, for the latter will nourish your soul

6. Breathe in deeply the Larimar light, and sound *OM* through your heart chakra seven times; this will draw Zadkiel's deep presence into your energy field

7. Rest and notice how pure force extends from your heart into the space before you, by seven feet (2m). As your force intensifies, imagine a beautiful TURQUOISE Orb ray of light emerging from the ending of your heart's ray. This is the force of the Angel Zadkiel's presence. Then rest and listen to the Oracular whisperings of this Angel's magical presence full of gratitude, security and comfort. As you meditate you will feel the supernal light of the seventh dimensional energies of the Archangelic kingdoms loving you and healing you by the sacred Communion with the Angels of Atlantis

Namaste

ZAPHKIEL

SACRED LOVER

"Great souls aspire to be enraptured by the all that is in love."

TWELVE

ANGEL ZAPHKIEL

The sacred orange-carnelian love-ray of this extraordinary Angel rains upon us from somewhere utterly supreme, from the core of the love-light circuitry of the Source. It is drenched in the compassion, ecstasy, romance and surrender of the cosmic order of the divine feminine frequency. It is transported by the phosphorescence of silver rain which resonates from the electrical frequency of the soul. It is suffused with the very breath of God. This is the force of the great soul that was once reluctant before entering the body of clay millennia ago. This is the soul that was then enchanted by the ecstasy of the seraphic music and faced only one choice – to be embodied!

The nature of this love-light folds into our physical world through varying octaves or degrees, to eventually cascade into our physical bodies if we are willing to be sweetly held by its love. This brings incandescence into our carbon beings, a force that literally slips through the space-time continuum and illuminates our path with sublime ecstasy. Therefore, Zaphkiel unerringly inspires us to acts of great love, encouraging us to feats of personal compassion and divine romance.

Zaphkiel, Zaphchial, Zaphiel, Zophiel or Cassiel – all these names have been used in the ancient texts – is the agent of God's grace, teaching that true compassion is one of the highest vibrational forces. For the essence of compassion is steeped in the inclusivity of unconditional love, the love that bubbles forth from the very spring of the eternal, and so this Angel is often seen through the mystical texts as a solitary figure, moving through the vale of tears and shadows where the weary, sad, and lost ones move, passing to offer mercy, compassion and love.

Therefore, when we feel at odds with the world, when we feel alone and in desolation, Zaphkiel always appears if we call. Thus this wonderful Angel reminds us of the love from deep within the Source, which so often in moments of isolation we forget. This Angel of Sacred Love encourages us to find true romance in life, surrendering to the ecstasy of passion, allowing ourselves to pulsate with the joy of bliss and in devotion to the Divine. This ideal of love has a unique splendour within the octaves of divine emission, for it tumbles from the centre of the love-fire itself:

*The time has come to turn your heart
Into a temple of fire.
Your essence is gold hidden in the dust,
To reveal its splendour
You need to burn in the fire of love.*

*You are the cure hidden in the fire.
Concealed in pain and sorrow
Is Your compassion and love.
You are not only in heaven,
I see Your footprints
everywhere on Earth.*

– RUMI

If we open our hearts and fully yield to these moments of divine passion, we may be amazed by what flows through us – for within these moments lies a sacred pact, rich with the potential for blissful love, beauty, tenderness, creativity and grace. All we need do is to yield to the impulse of the love-freedom rather than holding back from the dance of life in the fear that we will loose the object of our desire – fear of losing our rapport with God, what could be more strange?

On Atlantis, Zaphkiel nurtured all aspects of life through the creativity of the Universe. Zaphkiel gave glimpses of other realities, whilst blessings of divine order were bestowed on all. These imparted such sublime wisdom that spiritual growth was immediately accelerated, for Zaphkiel was the gatekeeper to the depth of conviction in the very essence of all things sublime, that is, love.

High Priestess Hathor

The glorious existence of this richly-loved Angel was fostered by the High Priestess HATHOR who, as a sensual lover-priestess, dedicated her existence to evoke life through the sublime passion of Earth existence. Her worshipping form was closely linked with the pleasure and creativity of beauty, bliss, sacred love, fertility and personal destiny. Indeed, one of Hathor's principal roles was to define the destiny of an individual, determining the life path or spiritual lesson that lay ahead.

The rite of 'soul contract' was dispensed through Hathor, through the priests and priestesses who served her as sacred vessels of her teaching. These anointed ones were her dedicated sentinels and played specific roles in the unfolding of each aspect of sacred love.

The Temple of the SACRED LOVERS was decorated with Carnelian, Ruby, Lapis-lazuli, Larimar, Pink Quartz and Diamonds. Within the loved-filled atmosphere of the Temple, significant festivals were conducted around the Sun and Venus. The latter is the sacred planet of the lovers and, in most of the Earth's cultures, is considered to be the sister planet to the Earth; after the Moon, Venus is the most brightly shining natural object in the night sky. Venus's bounty brought the secrets of love-filled bliss into the lives of the Atlanteans.

Zaphkiel governed the second Chakra which is linked with the definition of personal identity and the development of the I AM PRESENCE. This orange-coloured chakra defines the nature and quality of our relationships with all beings as with organic Earth life. It stimulates the issue of polarity through the balance of the yin/yang principles, allowing us to calibrate our relationships harmoniously through weight, space and time.

The sacral chakra is where our desire arises from, leading to sensual or sensory pleasure, and the force with which we maintain an understanding of our sexuality in the world. Through these forces, we develop an ability to give birth to new levels of understanding about ourselves: the way we relate to the world and to the substance of life in general.

During the end times of Atlantis, Hathor took the Communion of the SACRED LOVERS to Egypt and the Mediterranean, giving rise to the many Temples associated with Hathor's existence. One of the great temples at Dendera stands today in memory of her divine impulse, creativity and passion. Hathor personified the principles of love as the Priestess of beauty, pleasure, nature, music, motherhood and joy, and was considered one of the most important deities throughout the history of Ancient Egypt for, in truth, she was the personification of nature.

In faith of this, Hathor was commonly depicted as a human-headed woman with horns, cows ears and heavy tresses. On her head of horns was set a sun-disk accompanied by the Uraeus, linking the temporal sovereignty of the individual plane with a spiritual mission. Later, in Greece, Hathor was aligned with Aphrodite, and in Rome Venus – the Goddess of beauty, love and sexuality.

Gaze on the sacred icon that heads this chapter and you will see the figures of Venus and Mars. Their lovemaking has taken place and therefore illustrates the unique union between the yielding vulnerability and passionate ecstasy of the yin/yang bond. These two archetypal forces represented how the martial, warring strength of Mars, when coupled with the beautiful love of Venus, revealed the core antitheses of conflict and concord, hate and love, intemperance and fortitude, in all humans.

The key lies in the relationship between the two, and how the growth of love and trust may occur from the fusion of such a force. This cultivates a keenness of perception, resting implicitly in the moment of the creative product as an inspired union that eventually gives birth to a brand new idea.

Creativity is a sensual experience. It is an in-the-moment sensory experience involving touch, sound, imagination, movement, smell and taste. An artist engrossed in the creative process often feels the senses to be heightened to such a degree that the act is similar to love-making, where all perceptual channels are open and in heightened states. As the artist continues creating a visual image or a spoken phrase, finely wrought musical cadence or multiple sensory images and impressions may fully interact, impinging on the final work.

Try to cultivate the Sacred Lover archetype within yourself. Attempt to produce that keenness of perception and moment-to-moment focus that Hathor and Aphrodite invite – feel the arousal of the sensual, providing you with enhanced pleasure of life, particularly within your devotional pathway. Try not to be preoccupied with the outcome or goal, just savour the piquancy of each moment revealing pleasure.

Judgment and guilt erect obstacles to savouring the pleasure of arousal, whether these be within the awe of spiritual devotion, the extraordinary pulse of creative genius, or the panting breath of deep sensual love-making. If we inhibit our passion, play and pleasure, we prevent powerful forces from flowing through us.

Therefore, cultivating an interest in aesthetic form, whether this be in music, painting, poetry, dance or drama, we simultaneously stimulate all our senses, indeed our very 'wits', to achieve new heights of loving, and this opens the allegiance of Zaphkiel's divine work and aid.

Lovingly ask yourself how you wish to draw Zaphkiel's force deep into your heart, your soul and your body. The questions below will help to magnetize Zaphkiel's existence in your life experience, celebrating your soul's inheritance, and rejuvenating the ideals of your love.

The quest set here is to allow this Angelic presence to move through your body's cells, so that compassion, ecstasy, romance and surrender, just to name but a few attributes, are implicitly lodged within your flesh. Therefore, when you pray or petition Zaphkiel, the force of this wonderful Sacred Lover Angel will automatically call you to the purpose of your life's quest and, in so doing, your life will be immediately transformed through the force that lives at the centre of the Universe:

1. Are your mind and body open to reveal your soul's passion?
2. Can you easily surrender your heart's pulse in each moment, or do you hold back from its capacity by prescribing the outcome of each action?
3. What play or pleasure do you engage in regularly to reveal the creativity of your love?
4. Do you easily release the notion of control, and live in the moment?
5. Which aspect of your sensuality do you give full reign to in your loving?
6. Which sense do you think or feel with predominantly – are you kinesthetic, visual or auditory?
7. Do you live and work to feel your sensual and sensory nature expanding?
8. Do you live in constant awareness of the deep love, compassion and ecstasy that soars through the Cosmos?
9. Can you see the ideals of love being enhanced by the experience of romance?
10. Do you devote the actions of 'sacred loving' to God?
11. Which aspect of yielding, or surrendering to the higher vibration of love, do you feel is missing in your life?
12. If your life were totally dedicated to the path of Zaphkiel's sacred loving, what would the future look like?

Pondering these questions will bring joy, passion, inspiration, vitality, and excitement pouring into the substance of your life, as a light-being of the Universe. Conversely, if there is no passion in your life, if you aren't emotionally involved in your personal and professional process, if excitement doesn't throb through your veins as you reveal your spirit in the world, there is grave reason to suspect magic isn't living in your dreams. Please consult a practitioner or therapist who can help you reveal your imagination to yourself and then to the world.

Feeling is the language of the soul, and therefore being open to the cascading presence of love is to be caressed by God's eternal love. All we need do is surrender, and the moment we surrender is not when life is over, but literally when life begins. This sacred love means we begin to co-create with God, and the Atlanteans believed that, when they surrendered to God, they surrendered to something bigger than themselves, they surrendered to a Universe that knows what it is doing.

The SACRED LOVERS communion on Atlantis espoused these values, fostered by Hathor:

1. To always burn with the power of love, allowing love to enfold each moment full of passion
2. To take this passion and open a pathway of pleasure and play, that are then in turn dedicated to the divine
3. That the life of the Galaxy is richly teeming with infinite creativity, that may be venerated as sacred and blessed
4. That the Moon and Sun provide us with powerful evocations of how the male and female principles are balanced, and then equalized by the love-power of Venus
5. That the giver of sacred love is recognizing the well-spring of infinity through co-creating with God
6. A deep, passionate love for the evolution of all beings and life within the Galaxy
7. An utter belief in the surrendering nature of the Universe to Divine Will and the profound rituals that allow us to dedicate our lives to the Source
8. A profound awareness of how the laws of the universe support Sacred Love
9. The ability to stretch one's soul to the possibility of all dimensions existing within the Galaxy
10. A constant yielding to the powerful guidance of the Divine Mother/Father
11. A veneration of the eternal jewels of love, for the betterment of all
12. A loyal meditation of the principles of Hathor, in the evocation of her constantly fertile nature

An Angel Zaphkiel Story

I hadn't seen Joe for some time, and then suddenly there he was, handsome, cheerful, rich in bonhomie and yet, as before, an underlying sadness just a whisper away, lying beneath the surface of what his appearance suggested was absolutely fine! We exchanged robust pleasantries as we stood waiting to enter St James's Piccadilly, for one of those wonderful talks given by a stellar-talent from the USA. Thank heavens for Alternatives! [See www.alternatives.org.uk]

I hadn't seen Joe for about two years when he had first come to me for Clairvoyance concerning the creative reorientation of his career and relationships. We worked well together, and I had supported him through a major redundancy, a speedy turn around (actually in three weeks) through the successful manifestation of another more elevated position in an excellent publishing company. All appeared well, for he was destined to earn a good salary, was aligned with great promotion prospects, and engaged in the creative opportunity of meeting outstanding authors from a diverse spectrum of earth-moving subjects, zeroing in on the Mind Body and Spirit field.

We had then moved on to a deep exchange about his relationships and, although Joe hadn't been in a fully loving relationship for sometime – he had instead moved through a 'career' of short-time affairs – I was able to help him define his purpose and make a decision to create a meaningful relationship that warmly resonated in heart-centered soul love. Joe was extremely excited about this commitment, and we discussed the best strategy for its manifestation, using leading edge creation techniques regarding self-actualization. These forthright processes embraced the notion that we create our own destiny, and that all one needs is belief, faith and trust – feeling that the desired outcome is within reach.

When I next met Joe, again on the steps of St James's, I was overjoyed to see that he was not alone, and was introduced to his wonderful partner of eighteen months – it had taken him just six months to manifest a beautiful lady. The meeting was full of magic, except again for that silent whisper of sadness.

They both deeply desired a child, yet it was proving difficult for Judy to become pregnant. Spurred on by their conviction, and a faith concerning our serendipitous encounter, they decided to book in a session with me as we lovingly exchanged the vibrant connection between us. In a week or two, they arrived at my practice.

Through gentle inquiry, it soon became clear that Judy had experienced horrific rape when at Art School some fifteen years prior to our meeting. As a consequence, she had become pregnant and the traumatic circumstances of the incident meant she had felt compelled to terminate the pregnancy at only four weeks.

However, although child-less, this had not successfully freed her from the self-recrimination, self-loathing, shock and fury at her assailant. Soon after the attack, the assailant had been committed to prison after a prolonged court case which Judy gave witness to, and the Courts had convicted the man for serial rape of both women and men.

Judy had received little post-trauma counseling and was extremely vulnerable, so we immediately began restoring the fragments of her soul that had been splintered during the attack and the post-incident crisis. Then we identified each part of the personal power she had had drained by the traumatic action, each part of the emotional equation was explored whilst repairing the wounds, using Alchemy as a means to transmute the pain. Finally, we explored the karmic element of the strife she had experienced.

All the while, Joe held Judy in the conviction of profound love and, in light of his ardour, I observed the sparkling orange light of Zaphkiel around the pair, which was so beautiful. Therefore I introduced them to the notion and healing of this powerful angelic aid and, being so moved, they decided to bring Zaphkiel into each aspect of Judy's healing, so that the very challenging nature of what she had experienced would become identified as a gift, as a pledge to action, as a much closer relationship with the Divine, to experience the deep love that pours from the Source.

We ritualized these pledges, and the content of the vow Joe and Judy made that day was long-lasting and profound, taking them into the deeper recesses of the knowledge of sacred love. Thus the intoxication and ecstasy of the process increased their passion for one another, beginning to heal the physical and emotional wound that Judy had once experienced.

They meditated on Zaphkiel's power twice a day during their daily meditation practice, and felt the need to explore the Tantric aspect of their relationship which, once again, intensified the nature of their creativity. I introduced them to a ritual once used in Atlantis, to draw in the power of the Moon to increase the creativity and the passion of life, that the Angels have taught me and which was closely aligned with Hathor's creativity and magic.

In consequence, and as Judy was already a talented artist, she started painting out many aspects of her healing, which brought the orange-fire elements of Zaphkiel's love burning through her experience, in completely organic ways. These were the deep crimson-orange hues of burnt sienna and tuscan yellow. All shone and illuminated the expiation of the deep sorrow, the deep-seated conflicts Judy had up to this time experienced and never fully expressed.

After three months of this unraveling, Joe called me to say that Judy was successfully pregnant and that their prayers had been answered. In fact, the very night they conceived, they had both experienced a sublime ecstasy far beyond anything that they had experienced before and, during the heights of their passion, had felt the powerful presence of Zaphkiel filling the entirety of their bedroom, intensifying their love making, and healing Judy's womb. Intuitively, they both knew that a fusion of divine proportion had occurred, bringing with it a spirit that intended the joy of incarnation, even to the point of feeling that the soul would be a she-child.

I'm now a happy Godparent to dear Sophie, who is a beautiful seven-year-old Crystal Child. Sophie has brought such power to her parents, and in consequence their love has encouraged an abundance to occur that supersedes any hoped for glory.

Below is a prayer that Joe and Judy used.

A Prayer to Angel Zaphkiel

Dear Archangel Zaphkiel,

Please hold us gently in this moment through your deep and unending passion, and allow your sacred love to inflame our ardour to the heights of new love. At the same time, allow us to feel your gentle caress, so that we may pledge ourselves to heal through love.

Please see us as two who passionately seek compassion so that we may surrender to the greatness of your sacred love.

Please allow us the possibility of rising through grace to a richer sunset and sunrise so that we may marvel in the glory of the Source, feeling ourselves touched by the ecstasy of your divine nature.

And please bring all our creative outpourings opportunity to fire reaching a fruition of joy that transfixes our love

So be it.

Amen

A DAILY AFFIRMATION TO DRAW IN ZAPHKIEL'S FORCE

May I surrender
May I feel ecstasy
May I love through compassion
May I live in the romance of the soul

A MEDITATION FOR BECOMING AT ONE WITH ZAPHKIEL'S PRESENCE

1. Find yourself in a sacred space, whether this be a natural landscape, or your meditation room
2. Light a candle, burn some Cinnamon (Zaphkiel's scent or essence), and play ambient music to consecrate the space with pure, loving intention
3. Having consecrated the space, breathe in the intention to be in the presence of Zaphkiel throughout the space and, if you possess a piece of Carnelian, hold it in your hand or, if lying down, place it on your heart
4. Align your spine, and create a mudra by placing your thumb and forefinger together. Feel your whole presence vigilant, whether you are sitting or lying down
5. Breathe deeply with the breath-light of the universe moving through your whole being. Feel SILENCE, SOLITUDE AND STILLNESS, for this will nourish your soul
6. Breathe deeply the Carnelian light and sound *OM* through your heart chakra seven times; this will draw Zaphkiel's presence deeper into your energy field
7. Rest and notice how pure force extends from your heart into the space before you, by seven feet (2m). As your force intensifies, imagine a beautiful Orange Orb ray of light emerging from the ending of your heart's ray. This is the force of the Angel Zaphkiel's presence. Then rest and listen to the Oracular whisperings of this Angel's magical presence full of compassion, surrender and sacred love. As you meditate, you will feel the supernal light of the seventh dimensional energies of the Archangelic kingdoms loving you and healing you by communion with the Angels of Atlantis

Namaste

EPİLOGUE

We are such stuff
As dreams are made on; and our little life,
Is rounded with a sleep.

– SHAKESPEARE

Reaching a point of completion in the writing of a book brings a zephyr of sweet sadness as the act of forming thoughts and feelings through the written word develops a strong bond with the message appearing in print before one. It's like saying "Farewell" to a dear friend and, as we learn from our soul's journey, endings are always beginnings, so on this occasion the Angels of Atlantis represent an epiphany – they invite us to bring into creation a vision that inspires the whole universe.

As we move through the creation of Earth life, before completing our temporal journey, the Angels wish us to bathe in the knowledge that we truly are the stuff that dreams are made of. For we are 'star-stuff', participating in a Universe that is an inter-connected whole, rather than just living out the role of an observer through the drama of our pleasure or plight.

The Angels wish us to live this experience in the full presence of the thought, desire, passion, action, will and intelligence that creates the dream. Thus we hold the potential to alter the destiny of cosmic consciousness through the ripples of unified thought made conscious in the bravery of our hearts and in the ecstasy of our souls.

All we need is to be in constant rapport with the consciousness of the Cosmos, knowing that all is eternally interwoven with the circuitry of our love. For consciousness is everywhere and everything within the cosmos, just as consciousness is truly all there is and, therefore, we are of the consciousness that is all consciousness.

The acute awareness of the Angels reveals that we are cosmologically rare, that we hold the great gift of creative free-will as a precious jewel beyond compare. For right after conception, after only fifty cellular replications, we become a hundred trillion cells, and this is more than all the stars in the Milky Way Galaxy. Furthermore, in each moment of your life, your organs are tracking the sound, vibration and movement of each of the planets, because your body is in harmony with the symphony of the Cosmos. Your whole being is a compass that has the potential to navigate not just this life, but to exist in many dimensions simultaneously, as a way of deducing the ultimate destiny of creativity itself – the art of heartfelt love painted on the vast canvas of creation.

The Angels wish that we vision ourselves as luminous creative beings, engaged in the evolutionary impulse of the cosmos, becoming more conscious of each moment as a self-realized divine particle of time. For at this period of cosmological transit approaching 2012, when in ultimate purity, we may embody an octave of galactic love beyond compare – our physical presence is reaching a potential for transfiguration. This means that our energy field can expand within its atomic fusion to such an extent that we become like orbs of light – transformed like Angels within our own field of force.

Awareness calls us far beyond the tangled web of the current geopolitical, social and financial vicissitudes, as we create a new paradigm by restoring heaven on earth. This means we move to new light as quickly as we move from the deepest slumber to the world of waking by dawn arising.

You see, our bodies have been genetically designed to allow self-awareness to surf on the crest of Creation's wave, to allow a projection of eternity to be fully realized on the screen of humanity, fully interacting with the density of Earth's matter. In this, many have evidence of the One, for it is through this power that we may recognize our purpose, our calling, and our ultimate destiny.

Just as it was in Atlantis, if we embrace the vibration of love through continuous moments of heart-centred consciousness, with the degree of conviction that gestures 'love is all there is', we blast open the furnace of our spiritual foundry full of conviction, and the intelligent compassion of an ancient way of loving sears through our living. With this passion, a trajectory to heaven is forged!

Behind us lies a rough landscape of challenging definition, strewn with the debris of our growth pains, for we often encounter chaos when entering the depths of the shadow. But, when we have brushed off the dust of darker periods, we see that we are freshly illumined by the notion of our soul's loving consciousness in union with the divine – constant, eternal and forever brimming with the unconditional fervour of the passion that love and creativity bring.

Co-creation is the Angels fervent wish for us, as it already exists for them, and in the belief that collaboration rather than competition is the next evolutionary step for mankind. The Angels knew us before we became beings of soil and water. They wish us to be immersed in the consciousness of the great sound field, to live behind the words, to see that we are a prototype of a new cosmic species, part material and part solar. For within all humans is the vibration of the temporal and the eternal, as we are a galactic species that may span the gulf between the invisible and the visible, between the mystery and the explicable, between faith and doubt.

Therefore, through us, a new cycle of creation may occur, which brings new worlds into form, and that allows us to perceive we are reflections of a unique connection with the divine.

There is no star that exists, there is no planet, sun or moon, tree or leaf, plant or flower, mountain or grain of earth that exists without being a living form in experience of the original vibration. This is known as individuation, and arises from the great I AM THAT I AM. When personifications of these vibrations distinguish themselves, they move like shooting stars leaping out of the firmament. They move to experience relationship with others that have done the same thing, occurring before once more submerging into the unified field of light that is the ocean of the heavens, and that from whence the energy once burst forth.

The message of cosmology is distinct, and the story of the Angels is concise. It is to reconnect with the magic of the vast consciousness of the broadened vectors and silver highways of the galaxy. It is to help us recognize that human beings cannot travel into themselves without exploring the infinite reaches of eternity. For the Angels suggest that each vector of manifestation is an octave existing on a single vibrational continuum. When the octaves are lowered, they offer greater multiplicity of creation, whereas when the octaves are higher, a lessening of that creative form occurs, with a return to the singularity of being inclusive.

What creates the great diversity of creation for Homo sapiens is their ability to move freely wherever they will, as they transit these possibilities. It is within this force that all new knowledge is gained, because it is at this level of Earth counsel that the known meets the unknown, and the diversity maximizes such learning opportunities.

The Angels wish you well with your journey, praying and praising and, as they do this, each moment for you becomes a unique moment of love unfolding, as you sojourn the extent of your chosen incarnation. For this life of yours is a chosen path, unfolding as your soul decrees, bringing you moments of rare evolution as a force of spirited consciousness within the Cosmos.

The greatest relevance, developed in recent centuries of time, is the consistent evolution of global communication through the medium of the Internet and, as a consequence of communication technology, the education of the Angels has rapidly leapt forward, completing the promise of an age-old prophecy first scribed in Atlantis.

The more tragic scenarios of our transition into a post-historic order of being are, according to the Angels, no longer possible. Therefore, we might achieve the optimal objective of a free-flow, fluid transition into a new Golden Age, because a 'viral' response to planetary awakening could occur at any time. We recently saw such dramatic whispers of planetary consciousness during the early months of 2011, in the release of the old paradigm Patriarchal restraints, within the countries of Tunisia, Egypt and Libya, and beyond. Most significantly, within the surface energy of a mass-belief system that keeps many from the beauty of unconditional love, we saw a definite change.

Similarly, four billion inhabitants of Planet Earth watched suspended within satellite communications, viewing the gracious and surprisingly innocent wedding of two young people who became the Duke and Duchess of Cambridge. This was an unprecedented spectacle of imaginative combustion. For through their solemn, yet joyous, oath-making, these two young people created a force of love and joy that are positioned as oracular devices in all our hearts and souls. This was the stuff that dreams are made on, by which a greater freedom may be known.

We sit pivoted at the tipping point of a great meta-historical event, where those of our species are triumphantly made conscious, where mankind becomes kind-man, where the love of power becomes the power of love, and the love of life is never the same again. This will signal a distinct phase of human evolution, creating new paradigms, new boundaries, new management, new insights, and new loving – about which the Angels of Atlantis are our constant inspiration, and for which my deepest gratitude bubbles over in the fervent celebration of their truth, wisdom, love and constant unconditional loving support. May your dreams be always fair!

—Stewart Pearce
August 2011, London